BRIDGES
to the
Customer's Heart

BRIDGES
TO THE
CUSTOMER'S HEART

Commonsense Uncontested Strategies to Guarantee
Your Customer's Satisfaction: Outsell, Outsmart and
Outcompete the Competition by Doing the Simple
Things They Won't Do

PAUL UDUK

Order this book online at www.trafford.com
or email orders@trafford.com

Most Trafford titles are also available at major online book retailers.

Printed in the United States of America.

ISBN: 978-1-4269-6546-3 (sc)
ISBN: 978-1-4269-6547-0 (e)

Trafford rev. 05/17/2011

www.trafford.com

North America & International
toll-free: 1 888 232 4444 (USA & Canada)
phone: 250 383 6864 ♦ fax: 812 355 4082

WHAT BUSINESS LEADERS AND PROFESSIONALS SAY ABOUT BRIDGES

"...it's the best business book written by a Nigerian bar none".

SUCCESS DIGEST EXTRA

"It has to be one of the best books I have read and overall the most succinct on customer service in Nigeria."

CHIOMA NWAGBOSO, The World Bank Group

"... a wonderful book! I'm deeply impressed with the live illustrated experiences and the 'hands on' approach."

EMMANUEL EKUNNO, Executive Director, Neimeth International Pharmaceuticals Plc.

"Paul Uduk in my opinion, is one of Nigeria's most authentic experiential writers - tackling such a major business problem with a rare combination of tact, humour and professionalism. Bridges to the Customer's Heart helps readers shift their focus from what can't be done to what can be done. It reminds us of our potential as opposed to our limitations. I recommend it unreservedly."

RICHIE DAYO JOHNSON (RDJ), Founder, Richmond Johnson Academy

"The book is amazingly amazing!"

PEARL CHUKWU, Banking Operations Unit, Akin Adesola Branch, Ecobank Plc

"A colleague of mine saw my copy and has requested for his own. Maybe you should send two copies just in case."

OBEHI A. OKOSUN, Credit Analyst (Specialized Lending Dept), First Bank of Nigeria

"I just came across your book and you know what...AM WAOWED!!!!! Well researched and straight to the point. Paul in your book, you thought locally and acted globally. A must read for all that believe in great things"

Kanny Eni-Ikeh, Business Banking, Diamond Bank Plc.

"Great book!"

CHINONYE OBI, Team Leader, D-Tap Kiddies, Ikeja Branch, Diamond Bank Plc

"The lessons from this great book have not only opened my eyes to enormous benefits and opportunities enshrined in effective customer relationship, but have also given me the secret needed to succeed in all facets of life, business, career, family etc.' Bridges to the Customer's Heart is more than a book, it is a 'road Map to achieving success in life'."

YOMI ADENSON, Manager, Management Accounts, Promasidor Nigeria Limited

"I must confess that the book you wrote is a masterpiece. When I first glanced at it my mind went to the American inspirational writers. As an apostle of service excellence, I will read the book till the last page."

MUNTARI ZUBAIRU, Public Sector, Abuja, Diamond Bank Plc.

"Bridges is a handy, timely literary intervention for business success, with a view to entrenching global perspective. Practical, simple and objective."

F. O. BELLO (Mrs.), Head Human Capital, PCD Associates

"WAO! WAO!! WAO!!! I just could not believe it. Wonderful, beautiful. This book of yours will definitely make a whole lot of difference in marketing and retaining customers in any business."

JOHN CHUKU, Business Manager, Warri, DB Plc

"I got the bridges, it is a must read for everybody in this life that wants to succeed in whichever field he/she is in. I've made up my mind to use it as a training tool for my colleagues in the office. It's simply beautiful. Thanks so much for finding the time to put this together for the benefit of us all!"

OLUBUNMI AWODIPE, Business Manager, Diamond Bank Plc.

"It is a truly great accomplishment – truly deserving of praise!"

CHIGOZIEM ONYENEKE, Regional Coordinator (Lagos/West), Diamond Bank

''Couldn't resist, in fact, I had to jump to the last chapter to read the conclusion. Worth every minute!''

AMY IYK-ASADU, Business Manager, Port Harcourt

''The book is a masterpiece!''

EZE OHAJUNWA, RMO, South & East, Risk Mgt. Div., DB Plc

''Bridges is a solid blend of theory and practice, humour and wisdom. Anyone who reads Bridges won't give bad service anymore''

MARTIN UDOGIE, Publisher BottomLINE Newsletter

''The book is a veritable training manual for individuals, groups and organizations keenly interested in serving the customer passionately while in the process enhancing their bottomline.''

JUDE ANYIGBO, President, Fireforte Services Limited

''An excellent book – diversely relevant; it brings to the fore many of the service delivery issues encountered in everyday dealings and also proffers practical advice on how to improve our interpersonal relationships. Consequently, it is a must read for my client facing colleagues.''

WALE FATOKI, CEO TSL Limited

''Many businesses are searching frantically to find the magic formula to win the customer's heart. Bridges to the Customer's Heart provides the magic formula or if you please, the "how to" win the customer's heart. In a single word, Bridges to the Customer's Heart is a "necessity" for every business.''

INAM WILSON ESQ., Partner, Templars Law Firm

"Bridges to the Customer's Heart is simply a practical handbook for all irrespective of your profession or the job you are doing; be you a school teacher, pastor, usher in the church, banker, lawyer, groundnut seller or market woman. Full of practical tips on everyday experience on how to keep your valuable customers and make new ones. Should be on every workers desk for ease of reference."

OKECHUKWU OHAMBELE, Procurement Specialist, Mobil Producing Nigeria Unlimited

"Brilliant book, replete with practical ways towards having a share of customer's mind and an enhanced customer's experience."

NKEM OKORO, Banker and Marketing Practitioner

"Relevant, engaging, easy to read, full of anecdotes / real-life examples of strategies and success stories. Bridges to the Customer's Heart is truly a step-by-step guide to understanding how to engage customers towards delivering exceptional services that meet their needs. A must for the survival toolkit of every organization desirous of reaching maximum customer satisfaction and, ultimately, profitability.

TOKUNBO CHIEDU (Mrs.), CEO, Compass Consulting UK Ltd.

"Every service provider should strive to operate [with] the principles outlined in this book. You need to wow your clients if you must survive in today's competitive market."

PROF. ATIM ANTAI, Dean, Faculty of Basic Medical Services, University of Calabar

"I loved the book and it is still on my desk."

CINDY NOVOTNY, CHSE, CEO, Master Connection Associates, Rancho Santa Margarita, California

Dedication

To Tony Elumelu MFR…

…2006 African Business Leader of the Year (Africa Investor Magazine), 2008 African Banker of the Year (African Banker Magazine). Chief Ferdinand Alabrara (Chairman, Board of Directors, UBA Plc) said of Tony, "We would be hard pressed to find someone in Africa better equipped to serve as a role model and mentor for Africa's next generation of business leaders and entrepreneurs." Tony Elumelu has exhibited uncanny entrepreneurial spirit, very rare amongst Africa's business leaders. He snatched the then moribund Crystal Bank of Africa Ltd., literally resurrected it from the dead, changed its name to Standard Trust Bank Ltd. (STB) and powered it to becoming one of the topmost banking franchises in Nigeria before banking sector consolidation. In a development unheard of in the annals of banking history, except perhaps, the gobbling up of National Westminster Bank, a bank about five times its size, by the Royal Bank of Scotland, STB swallowed up the old United Bank of Africa Plc., a bank that was about ten times its size by balance sheet value. To make the development more palatable, the name UBA was retained post 'merger'. With a balance sheet size of almost two and a half trillion Naira and ISO 9001:2000 certification by the time he stepped down as Managing Director/CEO, Tony presided over one of the largest banking franchises in Africa with representation in 18 African countries. We are honoured to have the chance to dedicate this edition of Bridges to TOE, for embarking on his next chapter - total Africa transformation.

".......the question isn't whether or when to start striving for service excellence. It's how to do it. And here we have a confession to make. Though we've tried to simplify the elements of producing outstanding service, and their subsidiary principles, putting them into practice is never simple. On the one hand, all the elements hang together. The best infrastructure in the world is little more than a drag on profits if employees snarl at customers. The most elegant service strategy is so much hot air if it is not based on accurate measurement of customer expectations and corporate service performance. The most inspiring leadership can't compensate for a product so poorly designed that it breaks down often and it takes forever to fix".

William H. Davidow and Bro Uttal
- in the book *Total Customer Service, the Ultimate Weapon*

Acknowledgement

Since the publication of the first edition of Bridges to the Customer's Heart, there have been a groundswell of support and encouragement from individuals, far and near, institutions, private and public, and organisations, large and small.

My wife, Aret, and kids: David, Winnie, Socrates, Nightingale, Paul and Athenia have been the most raving fans. Arit my mum, brother and sisters: Prof. Eno Uduk, Edna, Mercy, Gaty, Cathy, Rev. Sr. Joema, and Lucy were right on their heels cheering. Ugoeze Sarah S. N. Anyaogu, my mother-in-law, Okechukwu Ohambele, my step brother-in-law, and Ngozi and Ijeoma, my step sisters-in-law never wavered in their enthusiastic support.

The band of friends was led by Opeque, Barr. Ime Ekpoattai, Victor Mkpong, Emmanuel Inyang, Joe Uwakmfon, Martin Udogie of Bottom Line fame, TM Jude Anyigbo, TM Inam Wilson, TM Amaechi Okobi, TM Kyari Bukar, TM Remi Abere, Mr. and Mrs. Felix Folawewo, and TM Richmond Dayo Johnson, who coined the phrase, "Bridges, the soon to be New York Times International Best Seller."

The rhythm of support from the banking industry was infectious. My then colleagues in Diamond Bank led the chorus with Angela Okonmah, Faustina Obi-Martins, Obinna Uruakpa, Victor Ezenwoko, Caroline Anyanwu, UK Eke, Chioma Okoli, Nkem Okoro, and Nosa Osemwekha conducting the orchestra. Throngs from First Bank, Fidelity, FCMB, Ecobank, Zenith, UBA, Sterling, Access, GTB, Union, and WEMA fired salvos and doffed their hats, adding tempo to the beat.

The last, but by means the least, were the men and women of honour that stood by me to make it all happen, most not even realising how much their words of encouragement provided the needed tonic that saw me to the finishing line. To mention but a few, Vice Admiral Okhai M. Akhigbe (Rtd.), Pascal Dozie OON (Chairman MTN), Prof. Anya O. Anya OFR (Former Chairman Spring Bank), Mazi Sam Ohuabunwa MON (CEO, Neimeth International Pharmaceuticals Plc.), Mrs. Stella Okoli OON (CEO Emzor Pharmeceuticals), Tony Elumelu MFR (Former CEO UBA Plc.), Ms

Ibiai Ajumogobia (Managing Consultant, The Daisy Management Centre), Chief (Dr.) Asuquo Ekpenyong (Chairman Davandy Group), Emma Ekunno (ED, Neimeth International Pharmaceuticals Plc.), Olutoyin Okeowo (CEO Metroploitan Motors), Ambassador Vincent Sunny Okobi, Ray Ekpu (Publisher Newswatch), Frank Aigbogun (Publisher BusinessDay), Ed. Akerele (CEO Food Emporium), Johnson Chukwu (CEO Cowry Asset Mgt. Ltd.), and Paul Usoro SAN.

Audra Wilson-Max at Brand Africa Project wondered why the cover of the first edition could not be made more imaginative and went to work at it. What she came up with is what you're holding in your hand. Isn't it beautiful? Audra you know I've always told you, you're the most creative person on the face of the earth and I'm lucky to call you my friend.

Now, the last word. One person made Bridges come out of my drawer for if after reading the manuscript he hadn't said "this book is great, arrange to send a copy to my CEO, Cindy Novotny, when it finally comes out", Bridges would have died a premature death. That person I can now reveal was Ikechukwu Okobi of Master Connection Associates based in Rancho Santa Margarita, California. IK, you started the journey, and the journey continues.

Thank you all, now and always.

Paul Uduk, Lagos

Contents

PART 2: PROMOTING SERVICE ZEALOTRY 71

PART 3: CULTIVATING CUSTOMER LOYALTY & RETENTION 127

PART 4: MEASURE! MEASURE!! MEASURE!!!   **143**

PART 5: MINING IDEAS EVERYWHERE   **161**

Prologue

This book's focus is on the simple things that you as an individual and your company can do to turn every service encounter into what Tom Peters has come to christian *WOW!* It's the type of service experience that you wish could last forever. You feel you could hug the service provider for making your day. That's the way you feel when you've had a truly great service encounter! *WOW! Experience* is indescribable. WOW! Experience is memorable! WOW! Experience is unforgettable!

This book is on *Service Excellence.* The ideas and approaches encapsulated in the *Excellence* concept (now used broadly interchangeably with *Quality Service*) have evolved over the years, from the purely statistical orientation (conformance to requirements) used by the pioneering fathers, such as William Edward Deming, John Juran, Armand Feigenbaum, Kaoru Ishikawa, Genichi Taguchi and Shigeo Shingo to the broadly attitudinal approaches of Philip Crosby, Tom Peters, Ron Zemke and Claus Moller.

My fascination with *Excellence* and how it could be adopted nation-wide began in 1989 after I read *In Search of Excellence*, the intoxicating book on, what else, *Excellence*, by Tom Peters and Robert Waterman Jr., published seven years earlier, in 1982. The enthusiasm was reinforced a few years later after I attended a seminar on *Total Quality Management* (TQM) organized by the Professional Women Bankers Association of Nigeria (PWBA), affiliated to the Chartered Institute of Bankers of Nigeria (CIBN). After the PWBA seminar, I wrote letters to the Military Administrators in the then 24 states in the country urging them to immediately embark on the journey to quality by setting up quality circles in their various states and volunteering to be the facilitator of the transformation. Of the twenty four, only one, Lt. Col. Jafa'ru Isah, the Military Administrator of Kaduna State, who later became Nigeria's military attaché to Washington DC, acknowledged receipt of my letter through his personal assistant, Dr. Shehu Lawal.

In the years that followed I devoured countless books and went on to write an MBA project paper on *Quality Customer Service* at the Ahmadu Bello University, Zaria, with First Bank of Nigeria Plc, Union Bank of Nigeria Plc and United Bank for Africa Plc as my primary focus. In the process and through keen observation of how small and medium scale enterprises conduct their operations and making careful mental and documented notes, I started conducting seminars on *Quality and Customer Service* and became a local guru of some sorts in the Kaduna area. My guru status culminated in the founding of *Kaduna Executive Roundtable* in 1994 or thereabout, where CEOs of small companies and professional service providers such as hospitals, architectural, law, and IT firms were brought together to consider *Quality* and how it could be applied in their companies. Regrettably, the *Kaduna Executive Roundtable* and similar initiatives could not be sustained after I moved to Lagos early in 1997.

After a seminar on TQM I facilitated at the then Habib Bank Staff Training & Development Center (now Yar'Adua Centre), Kaduna, in 1994, most of the participants had beautiful words to say about *Quality*. A few will suffice here. Alhaji Aliyu Iliyasu Kakumi, the then General Manager of ASD Motors commented, "*This should be extended nationwide. People should be made aware through TV, newspapers, magazines and any other means of communication. Long live TQM practice!*" Abubakar Y. Galadanchi of the then Habib Bank said "*I will advise that this course be given adequate publicity nationwide. It is of tremendous value not only to business but human development.*" For Taiwo M. Mesioye also of the then Habib Bank, it was "*In fact, it is the best and most informative course I've attended so far*", while another staff of Habib, Sulaiman M. Salisu affirmed "*Nigerians should as a matter of urgency make it an integral part of our culture.*" The late Zachary Muazu of New Nigeria Development Company (NNDC) wrote "*It's a revolutionary idea. It will go a long way in changing our society if implemented the way it should. It is really desirable.*" Oreagba M. B. of the then Confidence Finance Ltd., and the only lady in the group, commented "*I almost feel I can conquer the corporate world.*" Their comments were reminiscent of the comment attributed to John C. Marous, the then Chairman of Westinghouse Electric, when he was quoted in Excellence Magazine in 1990 as having said "*Total quality is the absolute answer to all our problems, professionally and personally in this country.*" Their comments were not totally unexpected for I was similarly blown away when I first started immersing myself in the quality concept as exemplified by my clarion call to Military Administrators nationwide to embrace excellence through quality customer service.

This book promises immediate pay off to those that internalize its essence. For a moment, recall Garry Marshall's 1990 film, *Pretty Woman*, co-starring Richard Gere and Julia Roberts. Recall the scene Julia Roberts went for shopping, dressed in her natty seductive pant, to reflect the role of a street girl she was playing. Do you remember the way she was treated in the first boutique she went to shop? The shop attendants simply ignored her. They considered she was not worthy of their esteemed and beautiful boutique. At the end, they only managed to tell her they didn't think she could shop there! She shyly walked away, wounded and dejected.

Now recall the envy on their faces, how their eyes popped out when Julia returned with her fully loaded shopping bags after doing her shopping elsewhere. She had by then changed into one of the new clothes she had bought and when she asked the shop attendants, 'remember me?', they just stared at her. They didn't recall that it was the same lady they had ignored moments earlier and had indirectly told to leave their shop. Remember what Julia Roberts said to them? She said, 'you lose'.

Worldwide organizations large and small in both the public and private sectors lose countless customers for the simple reason that they do not focus their everyday activities on the customer. The organizations may claim in their adverts or *creed, mission, value or vision* statements that they are #1 in quality customer service in the world. They may have large bill boards emblazoned with smiling, presumably happy customers' faces, and punctuated with the words *passion for excellence*. At heart such words remain hollow phrases. Just visit their shops or offices and what you experience will make you want to throw up. From the gatemen, to the receptionist, to the secretary, manager, vice president, you name it, the story is the same: discourteous attitude to the customer as the staff attend to customers with sullen, unsmiling faces. The directors, vice presidents, general managers, and senior managers are either in a meeting, going to or coming from one. To them, the customer is a disturbance. In short, they are internally focused

The greatest revolution since the industrial revolution has been the move towards greater concern for the customer in all business spheres. This development has been spawned by changes in the world economy that started being discernible in the middle of the last century, especially from the decade following the end of World War II. Since then, the world economy has changed so dramatically with *service* dominating, to the extent that we now talk of the service economy. Now every company is a service company. This contrasts sharply with the situation up to the 1950s when most companies engaged in manufacturing. With the advent of service comes the demand for better service delivery and a greater focus on the customer. This concern for the customer has revolutionized business and the entire world. Everything made now, from cars, to cell phones, computers, stereos, games consoles, beer bottles and even house designs are more feminine, attractive, sleeker and appealing. Whole regions, countries and businesses of all types are reacting to this new reality and positioning themselves accordingly to become in word and in deed, customer centric, in order to attract and retain an ever dwindling pool of fickle customers. Continents, countries, regions, local government areas, communities and individual companies ignore the signs at their own peril.

The world today is divided into two broad camps, with countries that have *Quality* in one and those without it in the other. Japan led the quality revolution, with America and Western Europe effectively catching up by the middle of the 1980s. They belong to the first camp. Nigeria and most of Africa, except perhaps South Africa, belong to the later. Most Nigerian companies, from the large, recently privatized utilities to the small 'one-man' enterprises, still run their businesses the old fashion way. A great percentage (call that 100%) have not discerned the quality revolution let alone embraced same. This is a sad mistake for the race for the most valuable customers is on. Martha Rogers, at the time a partner at Peppers and Rogers Group, a management consulting firm whose clients included as at then AT&T, Broad Vision, Fiat, Harley-Davidson, and Prudential Securities reminded business people and readers in **The Conference Board** article: ***One Customer at a Time: Competing in the Interactive Age*** to brace up for competition as '*Everybody everywhere wants your most valuable customers and will approach them from all channels and geographies in ways unimaginable just a few years ago. So, like it or not, yours is a global enterprise.*'

With privatization of previously government owned corporations, chief amongst them Nigeria Telecommunications Limited (NITEL) and Power Holding Company of Nigeria (PHCN), the birth of GSM telephony and the influx of foreign companies such as Shoprite, Avis (*We Try Harder*), Protea, things are already moving at breakneck speed, and the Nigerian economy is changing so dramatically, the woeful infrastructure notwithstanding. Insular, poorly managed companies that don't focus on or just pay lip service to their customers will die. There is good news and there is bad news. The good news is that it is never too late to focus on total customer satisfaction. The bad news, however, is that merely satisfying the customer is now no more enough. The customer has to be *completely satisfied*, before you have a sliver of chance of him or her ever remaining loyal to you and your company.

This book is written especially for the benefit of small and medium scale businesses and for all individuals who have anything to do even tangentially with providing service of any sort, either as employer, employee, customer or supplier. The book consists of what I call *Bridges*. There are altogether ninety two *Bridges* (ten have deliberately been left undeveloped for a total of 102), arranged in seven parts. *Bridge* is a metaphor for the changes, actions and reorientation that have to be wrought at both the organizational and individual levels in the struggle to get to grips with delivering service that surprises, pleases, enthuses and delights the customer, which would make her want to come back over and over again. The idea in each *Bridge* is self contained, and actionable, that is, they can be put to use tomorrow morning. The ideas are altogether quite simple but making the practice of them an integral part of the organization's genetic code is not easy. For the ideas to have any meaningful impact, everybody in the organization, from the CEO to the cleaner, must be thoroughly indoctrinated in them. The book is a down-to-earth manual on how to deliver no-nonsense customer service, the type we earlier mentioned Tom Peters calls *WOW!* Tom, incidentally, said he borrowed the expression from Stew Leonard of Stew Leonard's fame. It was Tom though that popularised the use of the expression and we dedicated the first edition of the book to Tom.

This second edition of Bridges is dedicated to Tony O. Elumelu MFR, former Managing Director/CEO UBA Plc. for his outstanding contribution to business development in Africa. Tony has now set his sights on the total transformation of Africa through The Tony Elumelu Foundation. As the Rt. Hon. Tony Blair, former Prime Minister of the United Kingdom commented at the launch of The Tony Elemelu Foundation, *"In an increasingly globalised world, strong political leadership must be accompanied by strong business leadership. The remarkable growth of a number of African economies has much to do with the many business men and women who have built strong, sustainable African companies able to compete across the continent and beyond. Tony Elumelu exemplifies these outstanding African business leaders, and his achievements in Africa's banking sector are second to none."* TOE roundly merits the rare honour of having this book dedicated to him.

To avoid the her/him mishmash, we decided to use the two words interchangeably, so you may see *him* and *her* in the same sentence. It remains to say that all mistakes, both conceptual and grammatical, are entirely mine. Now to the *Bridges*, we scurry.

PART 1

Modeling the Service:
SERVICE STRATEGY AND TACTICS

Bridge One

KNOW YOUR CUSTOMER

The first step in delivering great customer service is to select the market segment you wish to serve with awesome clarity, deliver the service with devastating impact, and dominate the segment with unchallenged supremacy. To deliver the service with unparalleled impact, you must *know the customer*. If you do not *know your customer*, you cannot serve him. You may serve him but he will never be satisfied, let alone delighted. You may even annoy him because you may be doing the exact opposite of what is important to him. If you don't know the customer, you may even be wasting money serving the wrong people or wasting money on the wrong things, such as expensive adverts. When you don't *know* your customer, the tendency is to conclude that the customer is *difficult*.

You even have books written on *How to handle the difficult customer*. Paul Timm in 1994 made a video on **How to Handle the Difficult Customer.** As far as I am concerned there are no difficult customers. Continually falling short of satisfying some customers should alert you to the fact that you made a wrong choice of customer selection in the first place and it may be necessary to let such customers go. As Thomas O. Jones and W. Earl Sasser, Jr. highlighted in their seminal paper **Why Satisfied Customers Defect**, Harvard Business Review, November – December 1995, "*Not all defectors should be retained*". With that I agree. However, the authors then went on to suggest that "*the unreasonable demands of unhappy customers*" that have needs outside the scope of a company's capacity to deliver can be a threat to profitability and staff morale. The authors didn't stop there, they gave names of two great companies that "*regularly 'fire'* " customers they are unable to serve well. Of course I disagree with the idea of 'firing customers' for nothing can make a customer *impossible* to serve. I believe the worst that can happen is a drunk staggering into your shop, say, for service. In that case just call Achoholics Anonymous to help the customer, who will return to you perfectly sober and become a great customer after his rehabilitation.

Assuming you have modeled your service properly and have selected the right customers, you should proceed with the clear assumption that no customer is difficult. What every customer wants is to be treated as an individual. Every customer has a temperament, what I would call *genetic make up*, that is specific only to her. Some customers are hot while some are cold; some want to be called by their first name while some prefer their last name; some are leisurely while others are more businesslike; some like to be left alone while some prefer your staying close, talking with them and answering their questions. The various combinations are inexhaustible. It is only after you *know* the customer that you can design and deliver the type of service that will delight him. The big step in tailoring service to the exact specification of the customer is often described as *mass* or *service customization*.

There are many things that you can do to know the customer, but the simplest is just to go out and ask the customer. The simplest reason many organizations have failed in ever coming close to satisfying their customers is because the quality standards they set are based on their own frames of reference. They base their decisions on their internally imposed standards and expect their customers to comply. But the real world does not work that way. In real life, perception is more powerful than fact. When you know the customer and give her what she wants, *exactly* the way she wants it, you tune into the customer's emotional world. You give what psychologists call psychological air. It is only after you have achieved this congruence that the customer can be happy. She feels happy because her internal clock tells her that you care about her as an individual, that you care about the way she feels. When the customer is happy, she can be easily delighted.

A delighted customer will buy from you again and again and again. As marketing experts would tell you, only repeat sales will enable you to make profits. Carl Sewell, the Cadillac Czar and author (with Paul B. Brown) of the book, **Customer For Life**, has estimated the life time value of a customer in the US buying automobiles to be $517,000 (about N74.96mm). You can also estimate the life-time value of a customer for your business. You only need to estimate for one month and project for a year. Multiply this figure by the average number of years the customer will buy from you, everything remaining the same. *Knowing the customer* enables you to grow with the customer and keep her for life. It enables you think ahead and be completely proactive in your relationship with the customer. Stephen R. Covey, author of the best-selling book **The Seven Habits of Highly Effective People** related a story about the reception his family received when they visited Singapore in 1987 and stayed at the Ritz-Carlton hotel. Denis Waitley, the modern day philosopher and author of several best selling books including **Being the Best** and **Empires of the Mind** had related a similar story when he said he made a visit to Bangkok in 1976. Now, staff of Ritz-Carlton would not have so excelled if they had not mastered the *Bridge, Know Your Customer.* In both cases, the customers were met at the airport and whisked straight to their hotel room. This was a proactive gesture on the part of the hotels' managements as the customers were saved the hassles of having to hire airport taxi in a strange place they were visiting for the first time. Ritz Carlton provided augmented service, reinforcing its reputation as a truly Five-Star hotel. Whenever you visit the Ritz Carlton for the first time, your details are immediately and meticulously captured and saved in the hotel's super efficient and powerful database and whereever and whichever Ritz Carlton in the world you happen to find yourself you're guaranteed the same level of service you got the very first time you stepped into a Ritz Carlton. In effect, the Ritz Carlton empire knows you as an individual. It does not matter whether you're in San Francisco, Johannesburg, New York or Tokyo. Contrast that with a Owerri Hotel Plaza where I stay any time I happen to be in Owerri, and I have been to that serene town more than a dozen times. Each time I visit Owerri Hotel Plaza, I receive 'the complete stranger treatment'. You have to complete the forms and answer all the questions: why are you here?, where are you coming from?, where will you be returning to? and all those other questions the SSS and God knows who else require hotels to ask all guests. The reality of these cases is that the customer is a scare resource and as such do not want to be treated as an ordinary commodity. Instead, he wants to be treated as an individual, king or queen. In the new dispensation, customers are becoming very sophisticated, highly educated and aggressive in their demand for quality service

At the very basic level, dealing with customers you don't know very well can cost you money. Two stories involving a bank and a finance house illustrate the point. The first happened in 1987 in Sokoto and it involved the customer of NACRDB, the government owned agricultural development bank. The customer applied for a loan, and while the processing lasted, he made it a duty to visit the bank every day. He became very friendly with the bank's staff and they let their guard down. The long and short of the story was that the man eventually got the loan - which was used to buy battery cages for his poultry farm. The loan was disbursed in installments, and mostly in kind. After the man got all the installments, he sold the birds, battery cages, the feeds and every other equipment, pocketed the money and disappeared into thin air. Till date, he has not been apprehended. Unknown to the bank, the man was a fraudster. The second incident happened in Kaduna in 1992 and was quite similar to the Sokoto case. This time around it involved NACB-CFC, which coincidentally, was the finance house subsidiary of NACRDB (now BOA: Bank of Agriculture)). In this instance, the customer was granted a first loan of N600,000, which was promptly repaid in accordance with the loan terms. It was the policy of the finance house to automatically renew loan facilities to customers that had borrowed before and repaid, and at a minimum of twice the previous amount. Being eligible for a second enhanced loan, the customer reapplied and did everything to show the finance house staff that he was a decent gentleman. He visited the finance house regularly, and often with his wife. The wife at this time was pregnant. The man always made a show of helping the woman climb the stairs. A second enhanced loan of N1.2mm was approved for the man. Upon collecting 100% of the loan the man disappeared into thin air with the woman. Full due diligence would have revealed that the man was indeed a crook. The pregnant woman was not his real wife but a paid accomplice. The Lagos address the man gave was fake.

Knowing the customer is applicable everywhere: whether you're processing a bank loan, dressing someone's hair, addressing a seminar, negotiating a contract or a pay rise, answering the phone, selling in the supermarket or selling by the road side. In all instances, it is critically important that you *know your customer* in order to be able to give the customer exactly what he wants. Knowing the customer enables you to do what marketing experts call mass customization. That is, in a mass market, you tailor your service exactly to the customer's specification. When you know your customer, you won't spend so much on advert sending the same message to everybody. Today, powerful databases that enable you to gather all sorts of information about the customer make it easy to tailor service to the exact specification of the customer. This is what has come to be called *knowledge management*. Take the case of bank credit officers. More often than not, they sit down in their air conditioned offices and "package" facilities for their customers. The more serious customers of course reject such loans for not meeting their needs so you see the credit officer going round in circles wasting his and every other person's time. In similar vein, the more opportunistic customers with less than good character accept such loans resulting eventually in bad loans in most cases. You toy with Bridge One, *know your customer* at your own peril

Bridge Two

PURSUE CRADLE TO GRAVE CUSTOMER STRATEGIES

Strategy is the peculiar or unique way a company chooses to compete or the specific actions and counteractions a company takes to beat the competition and stay ahead. *Pursue cradle to grave customer strategies* means that you have already thought about the customer (*Bridge One: Know Your Customer*) before you even start thinking about where you'll get money to start the business. It means you have identified a need and you have found a better, smarter, more intelligent way of satisfying that need. Gone are the days when the customer would come to you simply because you had a better mouse trap. Today every body has excellent mouse trap so winning becomes a matter of execution, that is, how you go about delivering your mouse trap.

It is sad that 99.99% of companies do not *pursue cradle to grave customer strategies*. More often than not, business people start thinking about money, often referred to as capital to confuse, before thinking about how they will provide service. Most often people set up a business because they believe there is money to be made. This approach often leads to disaster, and it means that anything you say about the customer is an afterthought. Setting up in business before thinking about how the customer will be served is the reason most total quality management efforts from Cape Town to Cairo and from Lagos to Mombassa have failed. You have to think about service delivery as an integral part of your business strategy and not as an add-on, something you put your people through on a Saturday 9 am to 12 noon training session.

The reason the Japanese have succeeded so well is because they *pursue cradle to grave customer strategies*. The Japanese are the ultimate strategists as Kenichi Ohmae beautifully illustrates in his hard hitting book ***The Mind of the Strategist***. Before the Japanese make anything, be it car, camcorder, video, watch, they will ask questions how the customer's interest will best be served. For a car, they will think about the safety of all occupants, including the kids. That's why safety belt will be installed at the back for kids. To ensure maximum visibility is guaranteed automatic defrost will be installed for the back screen and wipers will be installed for the lamps and the back glass. They will think of durability by making the parts snap-fit. They will think of your pocket by making the car fuel efficient. And there are lots more. Honda will even think about Lagos bumper-to-bumper traffic by making the rear view mirrors foldable so they won't hit that of the adjoining car or get smashed when the cyclist (okadaman) darts through the chaotic traffic. When you bought that Honda or Toyota car, I'm sure your major considerations were durability, fuel-efficiency, sleek appearance and general handling. Not long ago while at Parkview Estate, Ikoyi, I counted the number of cars in our office parking lot and it was 12/12 (twelve over twelve), that is 100% Japanese – 6 Hondas and 6 Toyotas. No American car! No European car!! No Nigerian car!!!

Paul A. Allaire was the President & CEO of Xerox Corporation when I started writing this book in 2000. Now, Xerox literally created the photocopying industry when it launched the first plain paper copier, the Xerox 914 in 1959. Having created the industry, Xerox thought it owned it. Xerox was over successful and by 1970 it controlled more than half the photocopy market worldwide. And what happened? Xerox became complacent. It turned inwards. Product quality collapsed. After-sales service became mediocre. The customer became secondary. At a time, it was believed Xerox machines were designed and made so they would break down after a given number of copies.
Canon, Ricoh and other Japanese companies however made copiers that would not break down. Their after sales service was matchless. They ate Xerox's lunch, and by the late 1980s Xerox was tottering on the brink of collapse. Xerox could only appeal to its glorious past to the extent that Xerox's ad jingle at that time was 'We taught the world how to copy.' Who cares? Fortunately before the last nail could be driven through Xerox's coffin Paul A. Allaire came along. He told the story how Xerox managed its spectacular turnaround. Among the many changes Xerox wrought, he said, was the setting up of a service team that compared Xerox's working hours with those of Xerox's customers, which led to the discovery of significant differences. Presto Xerox shifted its work schedule to meet its various customers' work schedules and this helped Xerox in many significant ways to claw its way back from certain and ignoble death. Today Xerox is back with a fully redefined strategy as a document management company.

By now I'm sure you are beginning to understand what *pursue cradle to grave customer strategies* is all about. As you can see from the Japanese examples, *pursue cradle to grave customer strategies* is not about gimmickry and grandstanding. It's about thinking through the small stuff. Thinking through the small stuff is the most important work of the CEO. Daily, millions of customers switch their loyalty from their former banks, shops, hairdressers, insurance agents, churches, dry cleaners, stock brokers, you name it, for the simple reason that the people in the places they used to patronize seemed not to care. Nothing can be as fool-hardy as treating the customer literally with contempt. It is the responsibility of management to ensure that the right strategy for customer care is thought through, adopted, nurtured and made to permeate the entire business. This strategy must be conceptualized and made an integral part of the business right from inception, before the doors are thrown open for the first customer to walk in.

Designing cradle to grave customer strategy and ensuring its flawless execution is the first work of the CEO. This *values* cum culture nurturing job is one of the few jobs the CEO cannot delegate. If the CEO does not show commitment to the values, his general managers will know he does not care and if the general managers don't care, the managers will not care and if the managers don't care the rest of the people will not care. The people at the top show they care by doing what Tom Peters calls management-by-wandering-around, constantly working on the system, leading by example at the front and in the rear, thinking through what might affect the industry tomorrow and taking preemptive action and often times being willing to change direction by discarding what does not work. Only pursuing cradle to grave customer strategies allows you to do that. Bridge two, *pursue cradle to grave customer strategies,* is the master key to the kingdom. That is why Toyota's philosophy is " *Customer first, dealer second, company third.*" That is why Toyota will ever remain one of the greatest companies on earth. Toyota recalled over 8.5mm vehicles in 2010, more than it manufactured in the whole of 2009. The scandal was so earth shattering that Akio Toyoda, Toyota President had to travel to the US to apologise to the government and people at the joint session of Congress. Despite its *woes* most Toyota customers polled at the time said they would gladly buy Toyota when next they want to buy a car. That's the power of quality. When you have quality, you command the loyalty of your customers.

Bridge Three

ADD VALUE TO THE CUSTOMER EVERYDAY

Bridge Three is straight forward, but is it? In simple terms it means giving the customer a little more than she expects. It's about innovation. The average *suyaman* knows it – any time you buy *suya,* the *suyaman* cuts a piece of meat for you to taste before he asks you the amount you want. It is called *jara*, Hausa for extra. How many times do they give you a little ice crème, or meat pie, or pizza to taste at Barcelos, Sweet Sensation, Tastee Fried Chicken, MR BIGGS, Tantalizers, Noando's or Mama Cass, the top fast food chains? Why not? Now, the *jara* may be a courteous smile, an augmented service, not charging for the carrier bag, the list is endless.

What is the cost of a small carrier bag? I reckon less than N10 per two thousand, that is about 5 kobo each! So why were banks not giving them out free until the late 90s? I recall a vivid experience in 1993 as the secretary general of the CIBN (Chartered Institute of Bankers of Nigeria), Kaduna Chapter. I'd gone to Habib Bank (now Bank PHB) Head Office Branch, Bank Road, Kaduna to withdraw N120,000 (about $3,500 then) to make hotel reservations for CIBN's impending annual dinner. I'd never before had the need for a carrier bag so I was mildly surprised when I asked the teller for a carrier bag and he told me I could not have one, for as he put it, 'the bank does not give carrier bags". I was stuck with N120,000 in twenty Naira notes denomination. What to do? I reasoned with the hapless teller that had I gone to a supermarket, they would have put my purchases in a carrier bag even if I spent only N100, how was it that I was not entitled to one for all the cash I withdrew for which the bank earned handsome commission on turnover of N600. Luckily, the teller was responsive to change and quickly arranged a carrier bag for me.

Now banks give out carrier bags freely but I wonder why it had not always been so. Given that the average price of a carrier bag is less than ten kobo, and the goodwill such gesture can generate is unquantifiable, why didn't banks do it all along? Why don't banks credit their customers N1,000 for every N1million they deposit in their account to generate goodwill and more deposits? Why do banks resist paying customers interest on current account given that it may not necessarily reduce their profit? You need millions of such symbolic acts of innovation that cost you literally nothing to unleash the goodwill of your customers. And how many organizations are doing this? Less than 0.001% of the ones I know. Why? It is against the *policy*. In his **Thriving On Chaos,** Tom Peters lamented the lackadaisical attitude of almost all American companies towards innovation when he thundered *"the reality is that millions - literally an unlimited number - of innovation and improvement opportunities lie within any factory, distribution center, store or operations center."* Tom estimated that such improvement opportunities could be multiplied in the magnitude of millions if the entire value chain, including the customers, suppliers, factory, distribution centre were involved.

My new auto-repairer that runs a workshop, Autovision, at Lekki, before he came to collect my car to fix a fault called me to confirm if it was the right time to come. When he came we test drove the car and he explained to me what he suspected to be the fault. The car came back with the fault gone, and the bill was reasonable. He gave me one week before he called to ask if it was the right time to come for his payment. He explained I could pay any time I was comfortable, indirectly extending credit to me. The day he came, the first thing he did was to explain to me what he did on the car the previous time and asked if the car was performing satisfactorily. He did not insist on cash, and explained to me cheque was ok as he had an account with Diamond Bank. You bet, I've been marketing the guy seriously to my colleagues. I contrast his attitude with one of my other auto-repairers that worked on my Mercedes 190 on the same problem over a three-month period in 2005. This mechanic even went to the extent of changing my ignition key! Three months and more than N80,000 after, the problem remained unresolved, only to be fixed by another mechanic by simply changing the part. The part cost N15,000 only!

"Value", Buzzel and Gale pointed out in their seminal work *"**Profit Impact of Market Strategies Study** (PIMS) "is the relationship between quality and price."* The authors inferred therefrom the direct relationship between superior quality, price and value, and the reverse, the inverse relationship between these parameters. If a customer gets superior value at acceptable price, they reasoned, the customer has got better value while on the other hand a customer that gets low quality at a high price gets worse value. Since in a market economy it's the customer that determines what constitutes good or low quality, high or low price, the authors concluded *"Who he buys from, and at what price determines who wins or loses.".*

Norman R. Augustine, President and COO of Martin Marietta Corporation writing in **Executive Excellence** magazine argued that the biggest obstacle to getting high quality and productivity in companies is uncontrollable bureaucracy. In his view no job or outside regulation should go unchallended on the yardstick of what he called *"value added, the 'where's the beef?' test"*. He then went on to conclude that the value can both be tangible and intangible. As an example of intangible quality, Norman cited *"quality of work life."*

Bridge Three, *Add Value to the Customer Everyday* means, in one sense, that you carry out value analysis of all the jobs you *do* for *the* customer. All jobs that add value to the customer you retain, and all jobs that add no value to the customer, you do not retain. In another sense, it means looking at all the *moments of truth* and thinking up innovative ways to creatively turn such moments into high impact moments to further cement the relationship with the customer. Take the case of restaurants. The average 'high class' restaurant serves bottled water for which they charge three times the price the bottled water costs in shops. Now, not all customers care for bottled water, either because of the high price or because at a point in time, especially in the early 90s, nine out of ten bottled water was fake. Fakers just filled the bottles with tap water and sealed them up. Faking killed SWAN bottled water. Well not completely dead, the brand has been reduced to a marginal player. Yet despite the glaring concerns, no restaurant would serve you boiled filtered water they individually guarantee. I would be glad to drink water prepared this way for that is the way I prepare the water I drink in my home.

Bridge Four

TREAT EVERY CUSTOMER AS A PARTNER

What do partners do? They run business together. They share profit in common. They trust one another. They keep no secrets from one another. They grow together. And when things don't turn out the way they expected, they share the loss together. They analyze what went wrong, why it went wrong and what can be done to avoid a repetition. Joe Girard is the world's greatest car salesman. The Guinness Book of World Records says so. You'll see the reason why Joe Girard is the world's greatest car salesman later in this book. Joe has real passion for his customers, he loves them and he treats them as partners. In **How to Sell Anything to Anybody**, Joe Girard (in association with and Stanley H. Brown) stated that he pictures the number 250 engraved on each person he meets. He says each person knows at least 250 other people he needs to know - people who could become his friends and customers, too.

Bridge Four, *treat every customer as a partner*, is the surest way to grow your business. If you see the number 250 engraved on every customer as Joe Girard does, you can insanely grow the business. The concept of multilevel network marketing or simply network marketing is built on this premise but it can be applied to any business. Multilevel network marketing simply means generating a new market from every last customer you transacted business. You do business with John and he introduces Peter who introduces Andrew who in turn introduces James who introduces Phillip who introduces Bartholomew ad infinitum. But why don't other businessmen follow Joe Girard's tested method for retaining customers?

The truth is that the average businessman approaches every sale encounter as a transaction rather than as a relationship. When you adopt a transactional approach to the sale encounter, you view every service encounter as a conquest. You see every customer as a *target*. When you adopt a transactional approach to business, you see every service encounter as a God-given opportunity to make a kill. At the end of it all the customer goes home thoroughly beaten, to lick his wounds. You may feel you have *won* but believe it or not, this is short sighted. An unhappy customer will tell at least 25 other people, who will in turn tell at least 25 other people and so on as the **Technical Assistance Research Programme** (TARP) studies found out. What you have done is that you have poisoned your business. As Joe Girard, the greatest car salesman on earth according to the Guinness Book of World Records, reasoned, *"if I turned off just two people a week out of all that I see, there would be 70,000 people, a whole stadium-full, who know one thing for sure: 'Don't buy a car from Joe Girard'."*

On the other hand, when you see every business encounter as an opportunity to build a relationship you act differently. At every such moment, you remember Joe Girard. You tell the customer I see you as my partner. You tell the customer, I view this one encounter as leading to other encounters. You tell the customer, I value this relationship. You tell the customer, I want to make this relationship last. You tell the customer, let us plant a seed and let us water it together. This is the mindset that grows a business. *"When you treat a customer so well that he or she goes out and tells five friends how great it is to own your product – that's when you are doing it right,"* says Scott Cook, Intuit's cofounder and chairman of the board, as quoted by Thomas O. Jones and W. Earl Sasser, Jr. in their *Why* **Satisfied Customers Defect**, Harvard Business Review, November – December 1995. In this wise I loveed Intercontinental Bank Plc's 2008 advert campaign that went **'Happy Customer!' 'Happy Bank!'** Unfortunately for Intercontinental, the management overreached itself as it gunned for ever increasing market share and got its foot stubbed, and the MD/CEO Erastus Akingbola sacked by the Central Bank of Nigeria.

Contrast Scott Cook's thoughts with the way Starcomms, the Victoria Island, Lagos, based telecom services provider treats customers that use its internet connection services. In addition to straight telephone services Starcomms also provides internet services. The company makes it a point to send out unsolicited SMS messages to its customers. In a typical day you may get five messages. But how does it handle its internet connection services? Somewhat cavalierly though there is a discernible improvement over what it used to be four years ago. Now you can top-up electronically, and the company will alert you three days before your internet services expires. The company in 2009 introduced a customer care line 0702 8000 123 and an email address: customerservice@starcomms.com. Telephone calls now do get answered and if you send an email you get an automated response. Starcomms should upgrade its after sales service unit, and rebuild it into world class standard. It's permanently flooded head office should be attended to. Starcomms should not be carried away by its Thisday Best Telecoms company awards, for as we know some of the awards out there are usually given to the highest bidder and say nothing about how a company is rated by its customers.

Bridge Five

HAVE A CUSTOMER SATISFACTION DIRECTOR

Tom Peters in the article written for **Executive Excellence** Magazine entitled **Excellence is the Exception** expressed the opinion that the abysmal state of affairs in American corporations where even common sense is a scare commodity has arisen over the previous forty years when "accountants and adminstrative people" held sway. With the focus on numbers that accountants and adminstrative people are noted for, common sense was not required and this resulted in total insensitivity to the market place. He concluded *"I'm saying that unless we keep close to the customer, even the best companies may fail."*

Peters in the same article expressed frustration over the ambivalence of people he meets at different levels in different companies who are for ever passing the blame for the lack of seriousness about quality in their companies. In a typical Catch-22 situation, Peters stated that when he consults with top vice presidents they blame middle managers below them as the stumbling block to quality in their companies. And invariably, when he meets middle managers they point fingers at top management as being the archilles heels of their organizations inability to make any headway in the drive for quality. Peters concluded by saying *"and so you have this horrible stalemate because the middle thinks that the top stinks - and the top thinks the middle stinks."*

W. Edwards Deming, the father of the quality movement emphasized time and again that *"top management hold the key to quality."* In one of his very last articles printed in the **Executive Excellence** Magazine, Deming, as in the past, stressed that: *"Quality is made in the boardroom."* Deming cited as an example a bank that failed and opined that the bank might have had top notch operations as reflected in excellent turnaround time, good rendition of monthly statement but failed all the same due to *"bad management."* Deming expressed frustration and utter dismay at the crass misundertanding of the whole quality concept. Organisations may want quality but all pursue it the wrong way by focusing on flavor of the month programs such as management by objective, re-engineering, downsizing, automation, and acquisition of ever powerful computers and softwares. Deming contended that all these flavor of the month programs were falacies as none clearly pin points the centrality of management, which as he constantly stated *"Quality is determined by top management. It can't be delegated."*

Deming said it all. Just as you have a finance director, operations director, administration or human resources director, you must also have Customer Satisfaction Director (CSD). It must be emphasized that the CSD must be different from the marketing director. The CSD is the person to ensure quality is driven to the top of management's agenda. The CSD serves as the chairman of the company's quality council and reports directly to the board. The CSD serves as the bridge between top management and middle management in the company's drive for quality. Unless this is done, you are going to have a lot of platitudes about quality but nothing will change.

Among the banks in Nigeria, Diamond Bank has gone the farthest in its quality service drive. The initiative was started by the Bank's first COO, John H. Hill, who was at one time the Director of Training and member of the Policy Committee of Saudi American Bank (affiliate of the then Citibank). The initiative was further sustained by Clive Carpenter, the next COO, and is today overseen by the CARE2000+ (Customers Are Really Everything) Committee. The Bank had erroneously thought that it would arrive at the service excellence holy grail by the year 2000, however, when 2000 arrived it realized that excellence is a journey, and not a destination. To resolve the dilemma, the bank simply added a plus (+) sign at the end of the last '0' in 2000, signifying 2000 and beyond. Today, the bank has put in place an advanced, touch button system for monitoring teller service and other initiatives are on. The Teller monitoring system enables you to vote instantaneously after a service encounter, to say whether you had a superb service or a lousy one. The bank still has a long way to go in developing an integrated framework for implementing organization-wide quality but it has begun the journey. It's time for all banks to start thinking seriously about employing customer service directors to drive their initiatives.

Bridge Six

FOCUS ALL DECISIONS ON THE CUSTOMER

In your relationship, it's inevitable that one day something will go wrong. The hallmark of the world-class companies that truly set them apart from the mediocre ones is the way they handle such moments of truth. Whenever something goes wrong the world class companies always decide in favor of the customer. They take urgent steps to recover. They take urgent steps to save the day. The also ran companies, more often than not, always decide in their own favor. I remember as a credit officer with the then Nigerian Agricultural & Cooperative Bank (NACB) in Sokoto in the late 80s, to stem the high incidence of bad loans in the branch, I designed a *Credit Application Form* that consisted of 12 pages and I was happy with my effort. This form was meant for small holder farmers. Ninety nine percent of them (call that 100%) could neither read nor write. Their loan limit was N5,000. My thinking then was that the form would be able to capture all information concerning the applicant. Upon showing the form to my colleague, Glory Udoh, now with Shell Petroleum Development Company (SPDC), she was quick to point out to me that even a World Bank loan application form would not be that elaborate. Looking back today, I can see clearly that this form was not customer friendly. It was not focused on the farmers, but rather on our internal concerns - high loan delinquency record.

The truth is, the majority of organizations always focus their decisions on their internal problems and concerns and the interest of the customer is hardly a factor. Some engage in outright self deceit. Take the cases of the following powerful Nigerian monopolies, Power Holding Company of Nigeria (PHCN) (formerly National Electricity Power Authority (NEPA) (the electricity monopoly), the Joint Admission and Matriculation Board (JAMB) (the universities admission monopoly), and the Corporate Affairs Commission (CAC) (the company registration monopoly). The service one gets from these monopolies still leave much to be desired. Instead of supplying light, engendering enlightenment and promoting entrepreneurship, PHCN, JAMB and CAC supply darkness, misery and frustration. While PHCN's electricity bills are always months behind, JAMB's candidates' exam result is always almost one academic calendar year behind. CAC may claim in their website and billboards that you can verify company name within 24 hours, the reality is that you can spend months for the website is hardly up. PHCN's marketing unit that prepares bills and the recovery unit that disconnects electricity supply from defaulting customers work in separate silos with the right hand not knowing what the left hand is doing, more often than not the utility company disconnects light from customers even when they do not owe. More often than not the 'service crew' don't bother to confirm whether the customer has paid (in the past 24 hours say), once a customer's name is in the defaulters list.

As for JAMB, it demands candidates to pay for exam results. Candidates pay as much as N2,000 for the result even though they have paid to sit the exam in the first place. The Board may deny that it demands 'result fee' from candidates but with the thousands of candidates massed outside their gates in Lagos and Abuja year in and year out the board's management should be concerned. Now let's face the truth, candidates pay 'result fee' to move on with their lives because they know that if they wait for the 'official result' they will miss one academic year. Contrast JAMB's handling of examination result with the way *The National Council on Legal Education* handles Bar Exams result. The Council publishes Bar Exam result in three national dailies within one month of the exams and one wonders why JAMB cannot do the same. JAMB has an official website from which exam result can be printed but universities do not accept result from JAMB's internet website. Since JAMB's turnaround time falls short of universities' academic calendar forcing candidates to pay cut throat 'result fee' to get authenticated result, the Federal Government through the Nigerian Universities Commission (NUC) should demand of JAMB to publish exam result in nationally circulated dailies and at the same time compel all universities to accept such result, 'subject to confirmation' when candidates receive JAMB's authenticated results. Needless to say universities can verify result directly from JAMB. JAMB may be a monopoly but as monopolies go, the Board may wake up one day to find out that more bodies have been approved to conduct university matriculation exam. It happened to Nigeria Airways, it happened to NITEL, it happened to ICAN, it happened to the Marketing Boards, and who knows, it may happen to JAMB.

Universities now conduct what they call Post-UME Screening Exams. For 2007/2008 academic year, University of Benin required candidates to buy N1,000 scratch card from 5 banks (First, Access, Intercontinental, Wema, Unity and UBA) out of the then 25 banks in Nigeria, and the cards were to be purchased from only 6 towns in Nigeria (Benin, Lagos, Abuja, Enugu, Kano and Port Harcourt). In effect, if you live in Maiduguri, you needed to travel to Kano, the nearest town, some 1400km both ways. The return journey costs about N3,000 then! If you live in Calabar, you had to travel to Port Harcourt, some 500km both ways! University of Benin indicated the scratch card would become available from 21 August, 2007 and, entries would close on 4 September, an interval of 14 days. As at 28 August, the card was not available in any of the banks in Lagos. To confirm I checked Intercontinental Bank Head Office Branch, 23 Danmole Street, Off Adeola Odeku/Idejo Street, Victoria Island but the card was not available. One candidate I know closely had to make arrangement to buy the card from Benin, at WEMA Bank, some 625km away, both ways! How insensitive can a University (call that people) be! Why do organizations deliberately inflict pain on their customers?

You may think that decisions that only favor organizations, not minding how they affect customers are peculiar to monopolies but that is not the case. Peter Ellwood, the then Chairman and CEO of the then Trustee Savings Bank (TSB), at a seminar held at Christ's College, Cambridge, in 1993, recalled that before TSB embarked on the quality journey, their mortgage loan clients were required to complete five forms covering 167 questions (yeah my NACB Sokoto loan application form was far more customer friendly!). That was not all, the form required clients to indicate their account number seven times, sign off five times, and they were required to attend four to five interviews. To whom were these processes focused, TSB or its customers? After TSB got started on its quality journey, the form was redesigned and the number of questions reduced to, guess what, 25, with the client having to input one account number and sign off just once.

As with every other decision regarding quality service, the question whether to focus or not to focus decisions on customers must begin in the boardroom. Top management must through policies adopted in the company ensure that all decisions are for the comfort and convenience of the customer. Staff must be empowered to decide in favor of the customer, but above all else, the culture must be such that staff are able to question *"the way we do things around here"* as Laura Liswood, a one time assessor of the Malcolm Baldridge National Quality Award puts it . The organization must put in place a system to evaluate all past decisions (things move at breakneck speed these days so evaluate all past decisions daily) and any decision that cannot pass the 'would we have taken this decision were we to take it today' test must be discarded or fundamentally amended to focus on the customer. Most businesses are vast operations so there must be teams dedicated to reviewing forms, templates, policies and procedures on a regular basis. Such reviews must take into consideration feedback from customers and trends, and management must be willing to rapidly implement the teams recommendations. Unless an organization has such a mechanism and staff are empowered to question the status quo, pretty little will change.

Financial institutions (Banks and insurance companies in particular) are the worst culprits for sticking to outdated business models. To open an account in a bank is never fun. Call that nightmare. People dread opening bank account more than going to the dentist! To open a bank account you need to know the name of your late great grand mother, have a driving license (whether you have a car or not), have utility bill (even if you are just visiting the country). You cannot make a phone call in a banking hall and you cannot put on a cap (only rouges put on cap). What arrant nonsense! Why can't I walk into a bank and submit my passport photograph and have an account opened right on the spot. Banks call their antiquated processes due diligence, know-your-customer (KYC) and all such. The Central Bank of Nigeria (CBN) and the National Drug Law Enforcement Agency (NDLEA) don't help matters in this regard for it's their money laundering war that is at the root of this customers' woe. Why fight the money laundering war through banks and not through the tax office. As someone that has worked in the financial services industry for over twenty years I find some (call that most) of the industry's practices ridiculous. I remember my deep frustration as a student studying in Russia (then USSR) in the late 70's and on a visit to Nigeria trying to buy travelers cheque. No bank was willing to sell me travelers' cheque as according to them I had to have a bank account before I could buy travelers' cheque! I finally bought the travelers cheque from the defunct Savannah Bank, then affiliated to Bank of America (it was not the travelers cheque that did Savannah Bank in later in 2002, it was politics, so don't ask me where is Savannah bank today). I also remember trying to cash my travelers' cheque at the local In-tourist Agency in Kransnodar, Russia, and being made to sign my signature a whopping 150 times until the signature matched exactly (call it 100%) the signature in my international passport, not minding that I'd signed the signature in the passport three years earlier and people's signature vary slightly as years pass by. Any wonder the USSR died?

Insurance is another ball game! No matter what you do, they'll always find a way to vitiate your policy. The insurance company will not inform you that the insurance man moving around from office to office selling policies is in fact an agent and the first premium goes to his pocket as his commission. The insurance company will not inform you that the agent knows as much about insurance as your grandmother knows about computer (that is next to nothing). The agent is only interested in his commission. Yet the insurance company will issue the salesman an ID card allowing the agent to deceive you that she's a bonafide staff of the company concerned. In 1993 I had a running battle with National Insurance Corporation of Nigeria (NICON). I'd in 1989 purchased their policy called *prosperity plan* that enabled you to cash in part of the policy every five years. The policy was for 15 years and to test how much reliance I could place on NICON I cashed in after the first five years. That was when NICON wanted to know the name of the 'agent' that sold me the policy. That is when NICON wanted to verify my signature. Why agent? Why didn't NICON ask any questions when I paid the premiums for five good years, from 1989 to 1993? The correspondence was going back and forth for six months when in exasperation I wrote directly to the then Managing Director of NICON, Alhaji Mohammed Kari. His personal assistant wrote to apologize on his behalf and shortly after that I received a cheque for N3,500! Three thousand five hundred Naira!! And the premiums I paid was over five thousand Naira! Where was the prosperity in the plan? More than the yield, the bigger question was, if it took me, the direct beneficiary, over six months to get paid, how many years would it have taken my next-of-kin if I'd died? Would NICON have written to my next-of-kin to inform them that their late bread winner had a prosperity plan and quickly arranged to pay? Your guess is as good as mine.

While Nordstrom is acclaimed as the quintessential customer focused store chain in the US, the following story indicates that the Japanese are still by far the masters in customer service. The story was recounted by Douglas D. Danforth, former Chairman and CEO of Westinghouse and he was being quoted in the Wall Street Journal. It told of an American tourist who bought a compact disc player in a Japanese department store. The customer was given a non-functioning window display model, just a box with nothing inside, and the customer only found that out when she tried to test the player at her Japanese host's home that night. Typically the story would have ended there. The customer would have waited till the following day to call or head to the shop to complain and all being equal, the shop would have tendered the usual apologies, replaced the player and continued with its business as if nothing had happened but not this Japanese shop. This is where the whole story really began. On finding out their error the shop's vice president was able to trace the buyer to her apartment in New York City using the information on the American Express Card charge slip and was able to get additional information on where the lady was staying in Tokyo and immediately contacted the elated lady. Before long, a team was despatched to deliver a working compact disc player, and as the story goes, "*a set of towels, a box of cakes, and sincere apologies.*" What a superb ending! The story went on to contrast the woman's experience in Tokyo with the one she had with a Manhattan department store that had made an unauthorised charge to her account and for six months the matter remained unresolved and left her unsatisfied. You don't need to go to Harvard Business School to be taught how to rise to the ocassion, to seize the moment when service failure occurs. Harvard may teach you the principles, but how to handle the day-to-day challenges that will inevitably occur and that will almost certainly tax your customer service prowess to the limits can only come from the fertile imagination of your collective mind and your management's resolve to always excel.

When in a bank and you are confronted with a bandit screen, how do you feel? Is it convenient to communicate with the bank teller through a bandit screen? Bridge Six, *focus all decisions on the customer*, is the key that will really enable you see how customer focused you are. It enables you take the view that the customer is always innocent even when proven *guilty*. You see 99.99% of customers are straight forward honorable gentlemen and ladies who want to do business with us in convenient, hassles-free setting. But because of the occasional problems we encounter with the minority (0.01%) of customers, who in most cases are merely being defensive, we put all sorts of obstacles on the path of the majority that at the end of the day, doing business with us becomes a sacrifice. Your objective as Chairman, MD/CEO, COO, GM, Vice President, Manager, Team Leader, Supervisor and what have you, is to reduce the customer sacrifice - the difference between the customer's ideal and what they settle for.

Bridge Seven

TRAIN YOUR CUSTOMERS AND INTERNALLY PROVIDE ON-GOING CUSTOMER SERVICE TRAINING

Today's management mantra worldwide is training. Your management consultant will admonish you to train your staff, retrain and train some more. Now that is not a bad idea for workers. Training is now no more a privilege but a right. These days you have prospective employees asking at the point of joining a company will you train me, and if you cannot give a clear cut *yes* answer, you have them saying sorry I can't work for you. In recent times, there has developed a second dimension of training requiring that you train your customers. Now, that is not an entirely revolutionary idea, as sellers of industrial goods have always had the training of buyers' employees as part of the contract of sale. It is however revolutionary in the context of service. The reason is obvious. The pace of change is such that if you do not in addition to your people, train your customers, you will not have anyone to call customers tomorrow. Let me illustrate how this is playing out in the plastic cards market of the financial services industry.

As early as 1990, many Nigerian banks were coming out with branded plastic cards and in the mid nineties electronic purse cards were added. Prominent among the former were UBACARD, FIRSTCASH, UNIONCARD and in the later category were ESCACARD by Allstates Trust Bank (now part of ECOBANK Group) and Paycard by Diamond Bank. Now ask any of the banks where the cards are today and they will have nothing to tell you. The simple answer is, the cards are no more. In the case of the electronic purses, a recent research has shown that the major reason the cards were abandoned was *ignorance* of the operators of the POS (point of sale) terminals in merchants' shops. It turned out that once the POS terminals were installed, the banks never bothered to go back to train the operators and when once there was a staff change, the new hire was completely ignorant and knew nothing about how to operate the merchant BTT/POS terminals and they were simply left to gather dust. If the banks had engaged in aggressively training the merchant tellers, who were the end users, in addition to their staff, as they were busy rolling out the products, perhaps the outcome today would have been different.

One would have expected that the VALUCARD consortium would learn a valuable lesson from the demise of ESCACARD and others. They did not and VALUCARD died a natural death despite the fact that it was supported by over 35 banks in the days when there were over 89 banks in Nigeria. The rival SMARTPAY similarly supported by over 35 consortium banks never really took off the ground and died more or less at birth. A valuable lesson to learn is that you cannot dispense with training third party vendors (customers) when their performance is critical to the success of your effort. *Interswitch*, the new kid on the electronic payment block seems to have taken off on the right footing with training high on its agenda. Hopefully the current strategy of generous training of vendees' employees will be sustained.

Bridge Eight

FIND OUT WHAT YOUR FRONTLINE STAFF KNOW ABOUT CUSTOMER SERVICE

Let your people go. Get management off the back of the people. This Bridge goes beyond empowerment. It means letting every internal customer, more so, the frontline people becoming the owners of the business. Yes, fully owning the business, as entrepreneurs.

Where are you most likely to get the best information about where your service is breaking down and why customers are not getting what they deserve? From your front line people! They are there day in day out. After a few days on the job, an average frontline staff probably knows what to do to satisfy the customer more than the CEO. Why not? After all, that is exactly why you hired (that word again) her in the first place. It is estimated that 80 per cent of customer service frustration would not occur in most organizations were it not for rigid controls, policies, rules and regulations from head office.

Tom Peters in his **Liberation Management** described the Union Pacific Railroad company as *'stiff, hyper-formal, bureaucratic, stodgy, sluggish, and militaristic.'* Peters described how Mike Walsh, the newly appointed CEO, wrestled with the rot he met at Union Pacific. According to the Peters, what prevailed at the UPRC was a *"Byzantine bureacracy."* In one graphic example, Mike Walsh, the new CEO described his experience while on a familiarization tour of the Texas Region. Before embarking on the tour he had two weeks earlier personally written to all the shops to be visited asking the managers to submit in writing questions to enable him know what was on their minds. To his amazement, he said when he arrived at the locomotive repair shop in Arkansas a notice of his coming was only posted on the bulletine board a day before he arrived. He later found out that even though the memo announcing his planned visit came directly from him, *"the manager of the shop didn't feel he had the authority to act on it."* Guess what he did. He sent the memo to the GM in Texas who returned it to him saying the matter was for *"mechanical department to decide."* Pronto, the manager sent it to the head of mechanical department in Omaha, who left it on his table for some days before *"okaying"* it and sending it back to the shop manager. As the CEO lamented, " *in the meantime, nothing happened."* Talk about organizational silos! In such a scenario where a manager does not even know how to handle a memo without referring it upwards, it is next to impossible for customers to get quality service. Mercifully, this sort of company dies out anytime the gale of change blows.

Thomas O. Jones and W. Earl Sasser, Jr. in their their widely acclaimed Harvard Business Review article **Why Satisfied Customers Defect** affirmed that *"frontline personnel constitute one of the principal channels for listening to customers."* For the frontline employees to excel in this regard, Jones and Sasser state the obvious, they must be well trained to *"listen effectively"* and must be sufficiently empowered to *"make the first attempts at amends when customers have bad experiences."* They further suggested that systems and processes must be put in place to enable quick capture and rapid dessimination of information companywide. From their research the authors also discovered that in excellent companies not only frontline staff but everybody in the organization as a matter of routine spend time with customers in the bid to knowing their needs better.

The ultimate in listening to customers is the new practice of getting employees seconded to customers' factories or offices to better understand how to serve them. The practice of seconding employees to customers not only allows for understanding of the customers' corporate culture but also serves as a tonic to revitalize careers of the staff involved. Sam Walton, the late founder and chairman of Wal-Mart Stores captured it best in his **Ten Rules That Worked For Me**. Under Rule 7, he advised managers to "listen to everyone in your company." Having set up one of the largest store chains in the world, the pioneer of megastore that espoused *everyday low prices* obviously knew what he was talking about. Listening to every frontline staff that have first hand information on customer's preferences, encouraging the frontline staff to talk about what they know Walton believed is *"what total quality is all about."* He continually drumed to his managers to *"push responsibility down in the organization, and to force ideas to bubble up within it".* His basic advice was the absolute necessity for managers to listen to their staff (associates in Walt-Mart's parlance). Sam Walton got it right! Any wonder Wal-Mart is today the most powerful store chain in the world and Sam Walton became the richest man in the world before he died,

Bridge Nine

SPEND *ALL* YOUR WORKING TIME WITH THE CUSTOMER

Your typical day begins at 7.30am and ends at 7.30pm (gone for good are the days when it used to be 8am to 5pm). 7.30am to 7.30pm are 12 solid hours. Take away 15 – 30mins break period and you still have in excess of 11 hours. Your success will depend to a large extent on how many of those hours you spend with the customer. Typically, staff spend ninety nine per cent of their time in their office while the remaining one per cent is spent interacting with customers. No doubt this limited time available for customer interaction is not enough to build long lasting relationships or do anything tangible for that matter.

Now this Bridge requires you to reverse the order you spend your time. Ninety nine per cent of your time should be spent with the customer. Doing what? Simple, passing to the customer information, building trust, giving your expertise, letting the customer know he can always rely on you. There are endless things you can do. Just keep your eyes, and of course your mind too. What are the trends, is your customer aware of the trends? Can you help educate your customer? What is your customers' current thinking? What can you, and only you, do to make a difference in the way your customer does business?

The idea of spending all time with the customer is gradually catching on with Banks. Airlines are the major beneficiaries of this new development. Airlines as we know are heavy consumers and earners of foreign exchange. To ensure they are always there when their airline customers need forex, some banks these days assign specially trained staff to the major airlines. Before Swissair pulled out of Nigeria, Diamond Bank assigned some of its operations staff to the airline, which it shared offices. The staff went to work at Swissair, handling all their foreign exchange transactions. The bank gained and life was made simpler for the airline. Diamond Bank is now partnering with

Turkish Airline. United Bank for Africa (UBA) is charting the same course and is now well entrenched with Virgin Nigeria Airways. At the ticketing counters at all airports which Virgin flies you will be surprised to know that some of the ticketing staff are actually UBA staff.

Now this *Bridge* requires clarification. Spending *All* Your Time With The Customer, as all other bridges you have to cross, is more of a mental attitude, than anything else. Sometimes, you need not be physically present in your customer's physical facility but let your mind always be present. Let it roam about, picking up sensitive ideas, and cues and transmitting them to the right quarters of the customer's business and your senior management. That way you become indispensable, you come to be regarded as a consultant and you can be rest assured, the customer will not do anything without consulting you first. I applied this principle while I was the branch manager of Diamond Bank, Uyo, and to this day more than three years after I left Uyo Branch to return to the Head Office, most of *my* customers still call me to seek my opinion before engaging in any business. I am always the first person they call whenever they have a problem. As I was leaving Uyo, one wrote a useful testimonial letter to me, reproduced verbatim below:

> *Dear Sir, what matters in this life is how much your life has impacted on other people. Be aware that within this short period you have been at Uyo, your life has impacted so much positively on many lives and families including us (sic). We appreciate you immensely and thank you for all your help to us. As you are leaving Uyo for another location of your bank, we pray that God will continue to elevate you to a higher level in your place of work. Please give our regards to your family when you get back to Lagos. Thanks and God bless.*
>
> Signed, Chrisvictor Enterprises.

As you can guess, I will frame this letter and keep it as a memento for my grand children. They might find it useful when they enroll in business school some day. On the other hand, I was completely disillusioned (call that pissed off) one day while still in Diamond Bank's training school by the general attitude of some of my colleagues towards quality customer service despite the bank's focus on quality and I penned the following piece. I wonder what poets would say as to the artistic merit of my effort, but here is how it went:

On my way to work
I saw the customer
I hardly paid him attention
I was busy thinking about my work

On arrival, the phone rang
After initial hesitation, I picked the phone
Who could it be? I mused
Must be that troublesome customer, I concluded

Is that PC?, he asked
Who is on the line? I replied
I'm your customer from LA, he said
With annoyance, I asked, customer who, why are you calling so early?

Don't you want us to settle down?
It's only 7.30, I let him know
Sorry, timidly he said
Sorry for what, I scolded

Work starts at 8.00, he should know
And here I'm the lord
I need your help he let me know
You should be happy, I answered you at all

Before he could say
My N100mm deposit matures today
The phone, I had banged
I was too angry, I must guess

These customers, who are they?
They keep worrying you, I must say
Now is 8.00, that meeting I must go
That way is my escape

That memo is now at hand
De-hired, the end has come
I must go, I thought I was lord
The customer is king, now I know.

The above piece was published in the second issue, 1999, of Diamond Bank News, the then in-house magazine of Diamond Bank Plc. Diamond Bank was one of the first bank's in Nigeria to adopt customer-centric business philosophy, elegantly captured in the bank's mission statement: '*to create a unique international bank focused on providing creative solutions to customers' business problems with an absolute commitment to quality*'. Spending all your time with the customer can be a distinctive competitive advantage. When you become always physically and mentally embedded in the customer's business, you can trust you will always be the first person to be called for advice. It is said that Neutron Jack, well his real name is Jack Welch, at the height of his glory spent up to 90% of his time with customers. Any wonder Time Magazine named Jack Wech the business manager of the Century? When you spend time with the customer you are growing your business, but when you spend time in meetings, some without clear agenda, you are killing your business, believe me.

Bridge Ten

KEEP PROMISES TO THE CUSTOMER

Have you ever taken a cloth to your tailor (fashion designer as they are now called) on a Monday evening and he tells you to come back on Friday evening and collect it. You get there by 5 p.m. on the agreed Friday and the man has not only not finished the sewing, he has not even cut the cloth! The man tells you casually he is sorry, that there was 'no NEPA' (Nigerian phrase for power outage), and to add salt to injury, he tells you moreover, he had a lot of work to do. How do you feel? Now you need that cloth for a wedding the next day. Obviously you feel disappointed, and helpless.

What about the auto mechanic or repairer? Does yours live up to expectation? The typical mechanic hardly keeps promises. It's immaterial how long you have known the man. In the recent episode, after my wife's car broke down, I called my local mechanic Jide to see to the car's repair. The matter was simple, so I thought. The fan belt had severed on a Saturday. Jide, my auto repairman (mechanic in Nigeria) explained that it was the alternator that led to the severing of the fan belt. The alternator, he asserted, needed to be fixed as it was malfunctioning and all would be well. Presto, he collected N3,000 on the Monday following to get the alternator fixed. Eight days later and without any word from Jide, the car still remained where it was parked, and the alternator had not been fixed. When finally I was able to speak with Jide, the man said he'd traveled to Ibadan, that I needed to *exercise a little patience'*. I 'exercised patience' for over three weeks before the car was eventually fixed. Always, Jide had a story to tell. Can I dispense with Jide? No! He is the best in the neighborhood. A classic case of the devil you know being better than the one you don't know. So I'm stuck with Jide!

Sometimes you call a colleague in another unit of your company to request for an important information or document and the guy tells you (call that a promise) 'I'll get back to you within the next 10 minutes' and that is the last you hear from him. When next time you call him he apologizes profusely and tells you he'd been 'quite busy', meanwhile the work you needed to do remains undone.

Nothing damages the respect and trust people have for you more than a broken promise. It's much better you don't promise at all. But when once you do promise ensure you keep your promise no matter the price. You always hear a legendary service story whenever you read an article about Nordstrom, the 100 plus old US super store chain. Nordstrom has a 'no question asked' return policy. The story is told of a customer who returned a car tyre to Nordstrom for a refund and was promptly refunded even though Nordstrom never sold tyres. It turned out that the customer had bought the tyre from a company that Nordstrom had acquired and the Nordstrom employee felt obliged to accept the tyres.

Nordstrom is an acclaimed service leader and a story such as the one above shows the extent to which the company goes to keep its promises to the customer. No wonder Nordstrom's customers keep coming back. Now contrast that with banks that promise you 5 minutes service at all times and you go to the bank and spend two hours and they tell you we are sorry, the system is hanging. The Bridge *keep promises to the customer* is simple and straight forward, isn't it? Next time you're tempted to make to the customer a promise that you don't intend to keep, think twice.

Now let me tell you another personal story. When I first arrived Lagos in 1997 and needed to buy a bed, my cousin introduced to me Papa Azeez, the local carpenter, who lived opposite her flat. Papa Azeez, my cousin told me was a very good carpenter. I thought it would do no harm to patronize the best carpenter in my neighborhood. With well intentioned camaraderie I requested Papa Azeez to make a standard bed for me. The specification was 6 feet by 4feet. Papa Azeez said the bed would be ready within three days. Well, when Papa Azeez brought the bed 18 days later, its length was 6 feet while the width was 3.5feet! Meanwhile I'd bought a 6 feet by 4 feet mattress! Papa Azeez blamed his apprentice for the 'mix up' and promised to fix the problem within a few days. It took him the greater part of one week! That resolved, I asked Papa Azeez to make for me other items of furniture. This time around the specifications were written down and Papa Azeez kept a copy while I kept another. Guess what happened? The day Papa Azeez was to bring the items, he came not with the items but with a measuring tape to 'clarify the specifications'! Of course I no longer trust the man as somebody I can rely on to make furniture for me. Not keeping promises to the customer can be expensive, very expensive indeed, to the customer, and of course to you the service provider, in the long run. You will lose the customer!

Bridge Eleven

DON'T PROMISE THE CUSTOMER WHAT YOU CANNOT DELIVER

Nothing destroys your integrity faster than promising the customer what you cannot deliver. This is the reason why management gurus advice us to *under promise, over deliver*. My advice is never promise what you cannot deliver and deliver exactly what you promise.

Small business people are the worst offenders in this respect. Whether you are talking about the tailor, carpenter, plumber, electrician, motor mechanic, the story is the same. They will not deliver on their promise. You have the motor mechanic who collects your car and tells you the car will be ready in two hours time. And you wait the whole day and he doesn't show up. If only they knew the damage that they do to their business reputation when they engage in this sort of behavior.

Bridge Twelve

GUARANTEE YOUR CUSTOMER'S SATISFACTION

Now this is where organizations get their feet stubbed. In their adverts, they shout on the roof tops *your satisfaction guaranteed or your money back*. But when fate compels you to have any dealing with them as you must of course, you find that the people are all mediocre. There is no relationship between their adverts and reality. The telecom companies are the worst culprits in this regard. Their service really stinks. In this regard there is nothing to choose from between Zain, Glo, MTN, Etisalat, and Starcomms, the front runners, when it comes to service.

Well, *customer satisfaction* is the essence of this book. Customer satisfaction carries 300 of the 1,000 points in the Malcolm Baldridge National Quality Award assessment criteria, a whopping 30%. In a recent year, as Laura Liswood revealed in her **Serving Them Right**, "*167,000 applications were sent out for the Award, 97 were returned and only the 12 highest-scoring applicants received a site visit.*" As earlier stated, thirty percent of the overall score on the MBNQA is based on company's approach to satisfying customers. In effect, you don't just go out to proclaim that customer satisfaction is important, you must document how you go about this and everything has to be independently verified.

The ultimate in pursuing excellence through quality is the up-front guarantee of customer satisfaction. When you do this, you tell the customer in black and white, when you do business with us, this is what you get. The company simply tells the customer, challenge us, and hold us to the test. Doing this instills discipline in all, from the CEO to the least staff. When you take this heroic stance, you are like a jelly fish in a bowl, you have no place to hide.

Swissair in the years of Jan Carlzon aimed for 96% or more of its passengers to rate its service as good or superior, otherwise it took action. Omega Bank, before it became part of the Sterling Bank Group, guaranteed customer satisfaction on the length of time the customer spent in the line. To enforce the policy, if a customer spent more than 5 minutes waiting in line, the customer was paid ₦1,000. The policy put customer facing staff especially tellers on pressure to deliver on the promise for I suspect ultimately the cash was deducted from their pay. In 2001 I sent an article on *Customer Intimacy* to Mr. Segun Agbetuyi, the then managing director of the defunct Omega Bank who quickly wrote back to thank me. To me this was a rarity among Nigerian senior executives especially given that the man never before met me.

The ultimate in providing unconditional customer guarantee is L. L. Bean. The first time I read the L. L.'s Golden Rule I was astounded noting that the company started operations in 1912 when there was noting like computers, internet, worldwide single dial telephone systems and fax machines to mention but a few of todays gadgets we take for granted yet hardly can scratch the service equation. I wonder if Leon Leonwood Bean ever received honorary degree of Doctor of Business Administration (Honoris Causa) from all American Universities for his simply stated business philosophy of *"sell good merchandise at a reasonable profit, treat customers like human beings and they'll always come back for more"* which is more eloquent than all the toms written in the past twenty years that TQM has been a fad. The whole philosophy of unconditional guarantee and challenging customers to *"return anything you buy from us at any time if it is not completely satisfactory"* to me was and remains a masterstroke. To drive home its customer-centric philosophy L. L. Bean further proclaimed "a *customer is the most important person ever in this office, in person or by mail."*

Well said! Customer satisfaction guaranteed, no ambiguity and L. L. Bean has been doing exactly that for over 80 years. Does your company guarantee customer satisfaction? Does your invoice read *'goods taken out of the premises cannot be returned"*? Do you have *''no refund after payment"* policy? Think again if you do! You'll surely go out of business. In his brief treatise, *Ten rules That Worked for Me*, Sam Walton the founder of the behemoth Wal-Mart Stores stated in his Rule 8 *''Exceed your customers' expectations. If you do, they'll come back over and over."*

Sam Walton admonished his people to give customers exactly what they wanted and challenged them to give a little more than they wanted. Perhaps not in merchandise, but smile, apologies, and prompt restitution for mistakes. He kicked against cover my ass attitude of managing with excuses. He concluded rule 8 by saying *"The two most important words I ever wrote were on that first Wal-Mart sign: 'Satisfaction Guaranteed.' They're still up there, and they have made all the difference."*

Bridge Thirteen

REAPPRAISE YOUR RELATIONSHIP WITH THE CUSTOMER EVERYDAY

The relationship between your company and the customer is like the relationship between a wife and husband. It needs constant reviewing, reappraisal and fine-tuning. There are literally million of things you need to reappraise in your relationship with the customer. Are you communicating enough? Is the relationship mutually beneficial? What can be done to improve the relationship? Is the customer very implicitly satisfied with your service? Is he unconditionally loyal to you? What can you, and only you do, to ensure the customer remains satisfied? The key to this Bridge is knowing the right questions to ask. The approach to adopt depends on the industry.

Take the case of a bank. Initiating the relationship is usually stressful. The customer has to divulge confidential information about himself and his financial affairs. A typical relationship, as Laura Liswood highlights in her *Serving Them Right*, involves the front office processes of opening the account, what most Nigerian Banks call *customer service.* This is closely followed by what banks especially in Nigeria call banking operations involving basic teller and funds transfer processes of paying cheques across the counter or through the banker's clearing house, issuing of drafts or manager's cheques, foiling fraud, controlling queues, managing standing orders, sending monthly statement of accounts, and making referrals to the marketing arms of the bank for cross selling key products. Due to the stressful account opening and running procedures, the average customer dreads changing banks except for very serious infringement. Accordingly you see many customers locked in unsatisfactory relationships. Such customers qualify as hostages.

Most banks do not know the status of the relationship with their customers, even borrowing customers, in a consistent basis. This accounts for the very bad loan portfolio of virtually all banks. A bank or two will claim bad loan constitute less than

3 per cent of their loan portfolio. Don't believe them. The simple truth is that such banks don't lend money to businesses and manufacturers in the first place, which accounts for the grotesque balances in the *cash and short term funds* in their balance sheets, relative to loans and advances. The reason for the high level of bad loans is not far fetched, all banks, except probably foreign owned banks, evaluate their staff on 'deposits generated' and not 'quality of risk assets booked'. If you bring in deposits you become a high flyer and celebrity of some sorts. Such *celebrities* are at a high premium in the industry and hop from bank to bank, attaining manager status within a few years without solid foundation. Any wonder they crash out within a short time any moment a genuine responsibility is entrusted to them. Reappraising the relationship involves keeping score, establishing where you're getting it right and where you are getting it wrong. It involves fine tuning the bolts, tightening in some places and loosening up in others. Sometimes it may require abandoning the old strategy 100 per cent, doing a complete somersault and heading in the opposite direction. In customer service and relationship management you cannot afford to stand still or the relationship will leave you behind in the dust.

Bridge Fourteen

STRIVE TO BE CUSTOMER DRIVEN

There are many forces that can drive your business forward. The customer is one. Technology is another. Information is another. But if you look at it closely, you soon realize that technology and information are really means to an end. The customer is the only end. Scott Cook, Intuit's co-founder and chairman at the time of the board it was that said, *"If you can't please your current customers, you don't deserve new ones"*

Why are you in business in the first place? What is your vision and mission? What compelling reason drove you into business? Is service to the customer a part of that reason? Everything we have said in this book aims to make you a customer driven company? Unfortunately there is no magic wand. Fortunately, however, others are doing it and achieving excellent results. You simply have to know that the various parts of your business are joined neatly together like a chain and like any other chain, the business is as strong as its weakest link.

William H. Davidow and Bro Uttal in their best selling book, **Total Customer Service: The Ultimate Weapon** stated that embarking on service excellence is not the primary issues but how to see it to a fruitful end is. The authors confessed *"Though we've tried to simplify the elements of producing outstanding service, and their subsidiary principles, putting them into practice is never simple."* To be customer centric is not for the faint hearted or lily-livered. Excellent infrastructure, what some egg-heads call tangibles comes to play, the service strategy which must be based on precise understanding of customer's needs or expectation and the organisations level of performance must be such that it can live up to expectation of what it has promised it will be able to deliver. The company must excel in design and all must be driven by visionary leadership. Unless all these elements are in place, the whole attempt may turn out a charade or waste of resources.

Hunt down the weak links in your operation and eliminate them. Regularly call in unbiased third parties to audit your operations and determine where your service is breaking down. Have a disdain for the status quo. Have the courage to say this thing stinks. In her Serving Them Right, Laura A. Liswood, earlier quoted wondered why banks fail to act despite the usual long queues they notice in their banking halls every Friday. Liswood posits that these recurring queues every Friday afternoon are tell-tale signs of weak links in banks service chain and they must have the courage to take action to repair them.

Thomas O. Jones and W. Earl Sasser, Jr. in their Why Satisfied Customers Defect, HBR, Nov. - Dec. 1995, quoted Horst Schulze, president and COO of the Ritz Carlton Hotel Company, the 1992 winner of the Malcolm Baldridge National Quality Award as saying that the aim is not just customer satisfaction but excitement and if they are very excited about your service you must strive to improve. Horst Schulze concluded by saying "and if you have 100% customer satisfaction, you have to make sure that you listen just in case they change ...so you can change with them."

Bridge Fifteen

HOLD MANAGERS DIRECTLY ACCOUNTABLE FOR SERVICE QUALITY

So what? Have we not been doing this all along? What about the annual or quarterly appraisal ritual? You bet it's not. Organizations carry out appraisal first of all to reward conformance and secondarily to reward performance. What is performance if not customer satisfaction and loyalty? But 99.99 per cent of all company appraisals don't capture these crucial parameters in any organized way. When talking of "performance", the typical organization looks first of all at profit or such like contributed by the staff or unit during the last quarter. Most rarely measure attitude to the customer. Most organizations forget that profit is a by-product of doing things well, the reward for past effort. It cannot guarantee the future. Only customer loyalty, repeat business can guarantee future streams of income and profit.

Marvin Bower, founder of McKinsey & Co. was quoted as saying *'any service organization that pays too much attention to profit deserves to fail'*. And Marvin Bower is right. Nothing can be more counter productive than making profits while your service is nothing to write home about. To ensure your future is guaranteed, reward people for being customer fanatics. Let every manager know that he will be appraised for service, both to the internal and external customer, above all else. Your vision, mission statements and *Service Charter* will become a huge joke if managers are not directly held accountable for service quality.

I was privileged to review the performance appraisal form of one of the leading banks a few months back and I was amazed to discover that out of 54 points, only one had anything to do with customer satisfaction. One over 54, that gives you 1.85% focus on customer! Now, this is a very "enlightened" bank, so figure out for yourself the attitude of the not-so-enlightened banks on this matter. As a matter of fact, banks appraise their people on the amount of deposits they generate and pretty much on nothing else. Nothing can be more counter productive. Unless you hold managers directly accountable for service quality, nothing will happen. And how do you do that? Look at your appraisal system! What do you appraise managers on?

Bridge Sixteen

MAN THE FRONTLINE REGULARLY TO CHANGE YOUR MENTALITY ABOUT CUSTOMER SERVICE

Are you the CEO of your company and you believe in customer service and nobody challenges your ideas about customer service? You probably have excellent ideas about customer service and deeply believe the customer deserves nothing but the best. This is the challenge to you. Once every six months come out of the executive suite, fold your shirt and man your frontline operation. Nothing will be more beneficial to your business than your doing this every six months, may be for just one hour. Five days in a row is even better. It will open your eyes and you will learn more from the experience how to achieve service breakthrough than you can gain at Harvard or from all those stuff your consultants have been feeding you with.

You probably think that the CEO should not spend his time doing this sort of thing. Well what should he be doing? Participate in *'strategy sessions'* and *'annual retreats'*, the latest fad? To what end do we have strategy session' and annual retreat*?* The aim of business as Peter Drucker points out is *'to attract and keep a customer'.* Every action must support this overarching goal. For every business, priority number one is customer. Market share, profit, return on investment, return on equity, return on assets, and such like measures are all lagging indicators. The only leading indicator is customer loyalty.

When they newly started their operations in 1989, every senior staff of Guarantee Trust Bank was expected to perform teller operation once every two months or so as part of their service drive. With their focus on service it was not surprising that within a few years of existence, GTB had built up an unassailable reputation in service leadership. The bank stumbled when once it took its eyes off the customer and went for market share. In a massive shake up in 2001 or thereabout to regain its bearing, GTB sent over 100 managers and senior managers packing. Tom Peters in his

Liberation Management recounted that when Percy Barnevik called the shots at ABB, he re-organized the 215,000-man strong company into 5,000 largely autonomous profit centers with average of only 50 people per profit center all staying close to the frontlines where the actions are.

It's ironic that most banks in Nigeria keep their most senior relationship managers in their Head Office and the so called regional offices while quite junior officers man the branches on the false believe that since they work in a net-worked environments such practices have merit. Nothing could be farther from the truth. As far as I know, you cannot shake a customer's hand through a computer monitor! When Louis Gerstner Jr. arrived at IBM in March 1993 as the new helmsman, one of the first things he did was to launch what he called '*Operation Bear Hug*.' This was barely three weeks after he arrived, and it involved the group of fifty top executives of IBM. Each of the fifty members of the senior management team was to visit a minimum of five of IBM's biggest customers during the next three months. The executives were to listen, to show the customers that IBM cared, and to implement holding action as appropriate. Each of their direct reports (a total of more than 200 executives) was to do the same. For each Bear Hug visit, a one-to two-page report was to be sent to the CEO and any one else who could solve that customer's problems. This was a major step to reduce the customer perception that dealing with IBM was difficult. It was an important way, Gerstner said, to emphasize that they were going to build a company from the outside in and that the customer was going to drive everything they did in the company.

If you really want to know about customer service, where the shoe pinches, send all your GMs, DGMs AGMs and Senior Managers to the front lines now and then. It will open their eyes to see whether the manning levels are adequate, whether customers are happy, and whether some of those policies emanating from the head office are helping the company's cause or not. To put managers in the frontlines '*would probably require a major corporate upheaval*' as Marc Rubin of Arthur D. Little dared to point out in Strategic Direction, April 1998. Writing under the heading ''*The Eleventh Commandment: Love Thy Customer*'', the article singled out MBNA, the Wilmington, Delaware-based credit card issuer. MBNA as at 1998 was the second largest lender through bank credit cards in the US, with over $35bn in managed loans. At $35bn, the company loan portfolio was bigger than the total loan portfolio of all 89 banks in Nigeria at the time. As we earlier pointed out, the pursuit of quality is not for the faint at heart, and flavor of the month initiatives may remain just that. As Marc Rubin emphasised in his article, MBNA's success arose from '*a 15-year commitment to its customers. The corporate culture continually emphasizes the role of the customer, with executives listening or answering customer calls for four hours every month.*" MBNA got it right! Overall, in the Nigerian financial services industry, Zenith Int'l Bank appears to be one of the few banks getting it right in this score as most of its key branches are managed by relatively senior managers. Diamond Bank after many years of flip-flop on the subject of whether their branches should be managed by senior level staff or not, in October 2008 took a bold decision of categorising its branches into A,B,C, with 'A' branches managed at the least by full Managers and above. This contrasts sharply with the situation before where branches were manned by all comers with the attendant decline in service quality and other parameters.

Bridge Seventeen

DON'T FAKE LOVE FOR THE CUSTOMER – HE WILL KNOW

The Bridge *don't fake love for the customer – he will know* is about sincerity. You can't fake sincerity. Neither can you fake passion. I doubt if you can teach passion. I, however, believe that everyone can be made to develop passion for a cause. Kevin Freiberg and Jackie Freiberg's book NUTS! is replete with dramatic stories about Southwest Airlines staff's passion for their customers. Typically, customers reward them with passionate letters of appreciation to Herb Kelleher, the founder and legendary CEO, who also served as the chairman of the board. In one letter to Herb, a truly satisfied customer after citing all the reasons she dreads flying, such as tiredness, duration of flight, time difference and the rest, she concluded her letter with the following praise on the flight attendants, *"They were the best I've ever seen. Professional and sincere. They really made a difference and I enjoyed them both."* The truly astounded customer concluded that it was clear the attendants loved their job and loved meeting customers. The service according to her was from the heart and it wasn't the type that could be taught or forced.

In the league of great hotels noted for their passionate service is Marriot Hotels. Just as Southwest Airlines, customers regularly write passionate stories about their experiences at Marriots. One of such stories was used by Marriots in its adverts years back and involved a lady who says she couldn't sleep without her favourite bedtime drink. She had called room service and the waiter had informed her there was none in stock. The waiter didn't stop there. To ensure the guest didn't go without the drink the waiter jumped into his car to get the drink. Expectedly, it took the waiter longer than 30 minutes so the guest was not charged. Marriot staff by their empowerment policy often go out of their way for the benefit of their guests. The lady concluded her story by saying *"it's the reason why I'll never tire of recommending Marriot Hotels to friends and colleagues of mine."* It was an absolutely ennobling and elegant story and it makes you want to check out Marriot any time you happen to travel. Empathy, heroism and the willingness to go the extra mile. It all boils down to customer-centric attitude and passion. These cannot be faked.

Bridge Eighteen

KNOW THAT EVERY CUSTOMER IS UNIQUE

Do you have one standard procedure for serving all your customers? If yes, you are swimming against the current. Henry Ford found that out the hard way over one hundred years ago. Henry Ford was the father of the automobile. Ford was a genius. He had the presence of mind to understand that for the automobile to overtake horse-drawn carts of the day, the car had to be 'cheap', after all, his dream was to *'democratize the automobile'*, for the burgeoning working class. Ford went about this with messianic zeal, producing all his cars in one color, black. When it was suggested to him his cars should be painted in different colors, he retorted, *"paint them any color so long as it's black"*. He decreed black color for all cars (Model T) made by Ford in the first 20 years, from 1898 to 1918. It was not until 1919 when General Motors, under Alfred Sloan, with its many auto color offerings nearly bankrupted Ford, did Ford Motor Co. started painting its cars in colors other than black. Ford on the brink of bankruptcy realized the customer always has a choice.

Now, we have moved from the era where the auto maker paints his car in the color he chooses and expects the customer to select the color closest to the one he likes most, to the point where the customer decides how the car should be made in the first place. In future, Faith Popcorn predicts, vehicles will be made *"exactly to the customer's specification. The customer will send his exact specification to the car maker, most probably, electronically, and will have the car made and shipped to him as ordered."* In future, no two cars will be the same, she points out. John Naisbitt and Patricia Aburdene in their **Megatrends 2000** similarly predict auto makers will create many different versions with each responding to a unique customer's taste.

The concept of tailoring products and services to the exact specification of the customer as we earlier mention is referred to as mass customization and is widely practiced by local delicacy joints in Nigeria. Near the former Federal Secretariat at Ikoyi, under the blue sky, is the point-and-kill joint, where a customer can select the life fish he likes and has it prepared as pepper-soup within minutes. This is yet to catch on with the established conventional restaurants but the trend is inexorable. As for cars, fish, so will it be with entertainment, education, and lots of other services as Alvin Toffler points out in his book, **Future Shock**. Whether you are running a restaurant, a store chain, a hair salon, a law firm, the tax office or a bank, your operations must be structured with the notion in mind that every person is unique. Even at the physical design level, you must make provision for the physically challenged individuals that move with wheel chair. Most organizations in Nigeria have no provision for the comfort of physically challenged people, unlike in the US and most of Europe, where even buses and taxis are designed with full provision for such people. When you design your office and service remember every person is unique and strive to create a unique experience for one and all. A tall order but certainly not impossible. I must confess what you are reading in this book is really out dated. Yes! But if you cannot do something as basic as satifying the customer, how do you hope or intend to excite the customer, a far higher proposition? In a recent research, customers were asked what they expected from world class companies and by far the highest number of respondents said "personally manages my satisfaction (59%), while "understands our business" came a distant second at 24%. Other expectations such as "is easily accessible", "solves our problems", and "is innovative in response to our needs" were at the bottom with 10%, 9% and 6% in that order. What strikes you about these figures? Let me tell you, "personally manages my satisfaction" is about the unique experience you go out to create for the customer. If you are not accessible, solve my problems, and are innovative in response to my needs, how can you manage my satisfaction. To manage my satisfaction, you must first understand, I'm unique.

Bridge Nineteen

TREAT ALL CUSTOMERS EQUALLY

Is there a contradiction here? Just immediately above, we talked about mass customization and said every customer is unique and should be treated differently. How do you even treat all customers equally when some contribute disproportionately to your profit? Some bank customers account for a big percentage of the branch's profit, some airline passengers fly more frequently than others while some shoppers buy far more than the average. For all these, they get compensated in various ways. The big bank customer gets invited to take coffee in the manager's office, the more frequent flyer gets registered in the frequent flyer club and enjoys huge discounts, same with the big shoppers who even gets attended to by the store manager personally. All this is fair and good.

The Bridge *treat all customers equally* is about the overall psychological air of the company in relation to customers. How do customers feel? Do they perceive that they belong by the way your people treat them. Time it was in the old generation banks when you had to know some body to be attended to quickly. You only had to beckon to your pal, hand over your cheque and get paid and you walked away while others suffered their fate in stoic equanimity, and sometimes cursing. Now that is giving way to all round equal treatment, please queue here, with a compliance officer having a close look and everybody queues up. If you visit on a rainy day the doorman brings you umbrella, no discrimination; some companies have customers' club to which all customers belong, some have customers' newsletter with interesting articles and features for all members. Yet in some companies, especially hotels, where getting parking space is a problem there are specially trained valets that assist customers to park their cars. You simply drive up, come down and the valet gets your car parked for you. All that nonsense to the effect that *cars are parked at owners risk* doesn't exist in these environments. This is the essence of treating all customers equally; it's akin to treating people with dignity.

Bridge Twenty

BE CONSISTENT WITH THE CUSTOMER

In customer service, you're either consistently hot or consistently cold. There is no middle road. The flip flop kind of service that is today hot, tomorrow cold and next tomorrow lukewarm puts a question mark on your commitment to serve. Consistency makes you credible. Consistency means that it does not matter when the service is taking place, it does not matter where it is taking place, it does not matter who is giving the service, and it does not matter what service you are giving, your company can fly the simple quality banner that promises Quality Every Day (QED).

The Bridge *be consistent with the customer* is also about integrity. Here we are not taking about systems integrity whether in the broad or narrow sense. Here we are talking about integrity to the promises that you make, for in reality, outstanding service is a promise. A promise to your people to be top dog service provider, a promise to be true to the customer, a promise to be true to the product, a promise to be true to the brand, a promise to be true to the wishes and aspirations of all stake holders. Can your *service* be consistently guaranteed across units, departments and divisions of your company, across countries and all the far-flung territories that you have your operations?

Bridge Twenty One

BANISH BUREAUCRACY

Is bureaucracy good? Yes, for the dustbin! Know that excellence and bureaucracy are strange bedfellows. How many bureaucratic organizations do you see serving the customer with passion and care? In Nigeria the when the electricity utility bureaucracy was called National Electric Power Authority (NEPA), Nigerians called it "Never Expect Power Always". Today in the bid to privatise the company the name has been changed to Power Holding Company of Nigeria (PHCN) but to most Nigerians it remains NEPA. So your guess is as good as mine. No bureacracy ever serves its customers with distinction, except perhaps, the Red Cross and Red Crescent Societies. Yes, and the Salvation Army. Alcoholics Anonymous too! And Doctors Without Borders! That's about all in the whole wide world! The truth is, these not-for-profit organizations are manned by volunteers and not 'staff' as your typical Ministry of Works!

More than any other person in the UK, Richard Branson has spent all his energies lampooning British bureaucratic organizations, like the (old) British Airways, and to prove his points, he has set up rival outfits under the Virgin Group. Branson believes in speed, urgency and simplicity. When next you see Branson, look closely and you will notice he doesn't wear tie. Tie is synonymous with bureaucracy and establishment thinking. All his business associates told Branson that the world did not need another transatlantic airline and Branson turned the *impossible* into a highly profitable business by launching Virgin Atlantic Airline. And boy, is Virgin Atlantic profitable! Branson thrives on contrarian thinking!

As Marvin Bower once alluded, though in another context, as organizations grow and become more successful, they tend to become more self centred, and with myriad of committees and high hierarchy. As a direct result of growth and self-centerdness, the customer becomes relegated to the background as relationship managers are saddled with responsibilities unrelated to their core duty of serving the customer. Bower no doubt was castigating bureaucracy. Unbelievable as it might sound, in bureaucratic environments, sometimes, you hold meetings to decide when to hold meetings! Take the case of Nigeria's National Assembly, for over one month the committee of the two chambers of the National Assembly set up to review the country's constitution could not meet as the members could not decide whether the deputy speaker of the house of representatives should be addressed as co-chairman or vice-chairman. That's how stifling a beaureacracy can be! Can you imagine the board of private sector company, say GE or IBM or MTN, not being able to meet due to the inability to decide how to designate one of the board members in pecking order to the chairman?

Jackie and Kevin Freiberg of NUTS! fame tell the hilarious story about Don Valentine, a former vice president of Southwest airlines. Jackie and Kevin were personally told the story by Herb Kelleher, the then legendary Chairman and CEO of Southwest. Herb was trying to emphasise his disdane for bureaucracy and how much premium Southwest placed on speed, action and the can-do spirit. Herb was describing the rite of passage or call it baptism of fire that Don Valentine the new marketing top gun that was hired from Dr. Pepper went through. At a meeting called on a Monday morning in one January to discuss a new television campaign Don was asked to lay out his plan for getting the campaign up and running and he began by saying scripting would be in March, followed by approval for the script in April, and all being equal the cast would be assembled in June and culminating in shooting the commercials in September. If 9 months preparation was standard for shooting commercials at Dr. Pepper Don soon learnt such standard was for the museum at Southwest. The story concluded by saying, after Don finally came to the end of his presentation Herb Kelleher spoke up, *"Don, I hate to tell you, but we're talking about next Wednesday."* It was then that the scales quickly fell off Don Valentine's eyes and as the authors surmmarised, he came to know just as other employees that at Southwest *"there are two kinds of people: the quick and the dead".*

The Bridge *banish bureaucracy* as you may have already discerned is about speed and a sense of urgency. The can do spirit has to be woven into the very fabric of the organization from day one. It becomes the culture and is communicated through heroic stories and sagas of the past. With this mentality, unshackled by bureaucratic slow march, employees are not timid about springing into action and doing whatever it takes to help the company accomplish an objective in record time as yet another graphic story also from Kevin and Jackie Freiberg's **NUTS! South West Airlines Crazy Recipe for Business & Personal Success** illustrates. The story was about

Southwest's expansion to Little Rock. On hearing that the airline was planning to go to Little Rock, a competitor airline that was three times bigger than Southwest tried to scuttle the move by also announcing they were also heading to Little Rock in what they described as *"a compressed time frame."* Herb ever the maverick who never shied away from a good fight whereever there was one despatched his SWAT Team to Little Rock barely 48 hours after the competitor airlines's announcement and within ten days Southwest was ready to begin operations at Little Rock! In case you don't know what an airline needs to put in place before it begins operation, this is what: you need to get departure and arrival gates, draw up a flight schedule, get your computers and servers up and running, buy planes of course, and decorate ticket counters. Southwest accomplished what needed to be accomplished within ten days, sub-leasing all available gates from Continental airlines and when the competitor finally arrived Little Rock, they found to their dismay that there were no gates as Southwest had secured all. Talk about matching action with words.

In bureaucratic establishments whether government or private sector, talk and inaction are always the orders of the day, action is always the exception. In Nigeria, Zenith Bank is no doubt the action Bank. It is not uncommon to see a branch of the bank literally springing up overnight on a street where none existed before. Jim Ovia the MD/CEO of Zenith bank has no stomach for sloppiness and inaction, as an ex-staff of Zenith who is now in private practice but still works on contract capacity for Zenith related to me on my enquiry how Zenith does it. Zenith has over 300 branches in Lagos metropolitan area (my guess as the bank would not divulge the information), Nigeria's economic powerhouse. Whenever a suitable location for a branch has been identified and a report made to Jim, the next thing he wants to know is when the branch will commence operation. While it takes some banks over twelve months to *plan* each branch development, a typical Zenith branch is up and running within a month from the date the decision is made to site a branch. Bureaucracy and profitability are common enemies. Any wonder Zenith is one of the most profitable banks in Nigeria today! Though Marvin Bower, the founder of McKinsey and Company was of the opinion that the list of 'primary goals' of a successful firm should not include profit. He felt profit should be subordinated to the overarching goal of providing sterling service. In his opinion if you did your work well the profits would come. He was quoted as going to the extent of saying *"any service business that gives a higher priority to profit deserves to fail."*

If you didn't know, Zenith's service is sterling. I remember my very first interaction with Zenith. That was around April 2007. I needed a debit card to pay Nigeria Immigration Service (NIS) for my international passport (only Zenith and UBA issued the card as at then) and had to go to the Zenith branch not far from AP petrol station at Awolowo Road, Ikoyi. I was attended to by Mariam Musa, one of the customer service officers. She was extraordinary. She was engaged in tens of activities at the same time. The systems as usual were 'hanging', but she handled every thing so meticulously to divert attention from the fact. Ever smiling, she came back to me now and again to reassure me that my card would soon be ready. I played along and pretended I didn't know what was going on. Finally my card was ready. It was now time to compliment her having satisfied my curiosity whether Zenith was up to scratch in customer service. When I told her she did a great job she appeared taken aback, and replied, 'Sir I'm sure if I came to your bank I would get a higher standard of service, thanks all the same." That is not the end of the story. Within an hour I received an email from Zenith inquiring whether everything went well. No wonder, in Nigeria today, to own a Zenith bank account is a status symbol.

Both Peter Drucker and Joseph Schumpeter have in different contexts decried bureaucracy. Both men have said that *"retaining the spirit of entrepreneurship is accomplished primarily by defying tradition, challenging orthodoxy, breaking up the old, selecting niches, and recognizing that bureaucracy and success are irreconcilable."*

Bridge Twenty Two

PROVIDE EXCELLENT SERVICE TO THE NEXT STAFF, HE'S ALSO A CUSTOMER

A typical organization comprises units, departments, divisions, groups or whatever you wish to call the functions. Thus you have the Accounting Division., Financial Control Dept., Human Resources Group., Admin. Unit., and what have you. These units are designed for the smooth running of the organization and believe it or not they are all internally focused. They are all a throw back to Henry Ford's specialization or division of labor idea of the nineteenth century. In serving the customer however, you notice that you deliver service across boundaries. One dept. cannot serve the customer without support in the form of information from other depts. any more than you can serve omelet without breaking an egg. But what do you see in practice? Most senior managers run their dept. as their personal estates or fiefdoms, they hoard information, and they try their utmost to undermine co-managers. Information is power, the more you hoard it the more power you have, so it seems. Unless this type of mindset is quashed, the organization is in a state of constant tension, fighting interminable wars as managers jostle for power.

As with all other ideas in this book, the key to achieving the goal of serving internal customers with equal passion as the external customers is *senior management*. Senior management is the custodian of the culture, senior management designs the reward system, etc. The culture must engender open communication (what Jack Welch calls candor) and free flow of information at all levels and the reward system must be such that champions of quality internal customer care are handsomely rewarded. With the advent of the intranet, chat rooms, blogs and all other forms of technology enabled communication systems, the task of serving the internal customer with zeal and passion is made even easier. Zapping the information to the other staff is just a mouse click away. But be warned, the computer is no substitute to regular meetings where areas of friction can easily be ironed out. After all, you cannot shake your colleague's hands through the computer monitor.

No company can succeed without a good leader. David Ogilvy viewed the leader's primary role as "*providing an environment in which creative people can do useful work.*" Max Depree in his book on leadership said that the function of the leader is "*to give others the space to be what they can be.*" He said futher "if they approach their individual potential, so will the organization." He also said that "*the first responsibility of the leader is to define reality, while the last is to say thank you.*" Warren Bennis has said that what is pivotal for the leader is "*to have an overreaching vision, to set an example of passion, curiosity, integrity, and daring for the others in the organization.*"

Marvin Bower who we have quoted time and again in this book wrote so much about the firm and was emphatic on the level of professionalism he expected from the staff when he said "*It (*that is the firm*) never permits any relaxation of professionalism or of high standard.* He further went on to say "*This reality calls for constant communication both within and outside of the organization, relative to the goals of the organization.*" It was for this same reason that J. P. Morgan once said, '*the goal is to do a first-class business in a first-class way.* " For the organization to excel and succeed on a sustainable basis, the level of service delivery to the internal customers must be of the highest quality as that to the external customers.

Bridge Twenty Three

ASK THE CUSTOMER WHAT YOU CAN DO TO ENRICH THE RELATIONSHIP TOMORROW

Listen to the customer or perish! It's that simple. Perhaps one of the most difficult things to do is to seek to enrich the relationship when the market is booming and you control 80 per cent of it like IBM did in computers and Ford and then GM in cars. Back at home in Nigeria, you can recall that *SWAN* 'owned' the market for bottled water. *SWAN* water was as a matter of fact synonymous with bottled water. If you wanted bottled water you requested for *SWAN* , it didn't matter if what you had in mind was Ragolis, or Yankari. It's exactly when you believe you own the market that you should go all out to enrich the relationship, create loyalty and discourage interlopers.

Organizations that have got it right at enriching relationships create loyalty that is sometimes almost akin to cult membership. Customers are almost fanatical about them; think of Nike in casual shoes, Levi Straus in jeans, MBCN in financial services and Harley Davidson in motorbikes, to mention a few. How have these companies managed to create this sense of loyalty to their products and to their companies? Is there some magic formula? None I know of other than constant spirit of experimenting, searching, asking, creativity, unending innovation and the willingness to dare.

Bridge Twenty Four

BE COMPLETELY PREDICTABLE WHEN IT COMES TO CUSTOMER SERVICE

If you bought two Mercedes Benz cars of the same year of manufacture and model, you would expect them to perform the same. The same thing applies to service. McDonalds is perhaps the organization that has gone the farthest in striving for the ultimate standardization. First you have the double arch. Anywhere in the world you go the double arch proclaims McDonalds. Then you have the hamburgers and all the other quintessence McDonalds stuff. Anywhere you go they have the same tingly taste. And when you are at McDonalds, you can be sure of genuine smiles and warmth. Predictability sets McDonalds apart.

And if McDonalds can do it why can't MR. BIGGS, Tantalizers, Pintos (of bygone years), Tastee Fried Chicken, Chicken Republic, Barcelos, Sweet Sensation, Mama Cass, Kingstine-Jo, Nandos and the many others here in Nigeria? In all these places, their ice cream taste different every day, their people are sullen and nothing is ever predictable.

Just the other day I stopped at Nandos, Isaac John Steet, Ikeja GRA, to have a feel of the place. I was there about a year or two earlier and left with a sour taste in my mouth. This time around their vegetable salad was perfect. Their salad dressing is one of the best I've tasted. Guess what, a few days later when I went back for the salad, they had none available and it was just 8.50pm on a Saturday night. Fried rice was equally not available. When I asked the guy that looked like the supervisor why there was no salad and fried rice at 8.50pm on a Saturday night he stared at me sheepishly. I drove just a block away to Barcelos and got what I wanted. I spent N2,200 (about $14 - $18 depending on the prevailing exchange rate). Barcelos' gain was Nandos' loss. Now I have a story, anytime my kids or wife venture out for fast food I tell them don't go to Nandos, they are not predictable. To my friends and colleagues in the office, it's the same, don't go to Nandos, they are not predictable. As Joe Girard, earlier mentioned said, every person knows at least 250 people, who in turn know at least 250 other people. Add it up and you have over 70,000 people, a stadium full, who at the end would know one bad thing about Nandos: they are not predictable. And as we predicted in the first edition of Bridges, the gods of quality struck. Nandos on Isaac John street closed down barely barely six months after Bridges was published. You cannot afford to be unpredictable.

Bridge Twenty Five

DON'T PRAISE YOURSELF, LET THE CUSTOMER PRAISE YOU

The lizard that jumps from the 100-foot high iroko tree may praise itself since no one else would praise it but as a quality minded company you have to resist the temptation to praise yourself. Let your service do the praising. Be modest enough to admit you're still learning.

A little less than five years after they were declared *Excellent*, most of the excellent companies in *In Search* started down the road to extinction. Twenty years on, some of the once excellent companies are all but shadows of their former selves. Wang Computers for example failed just a few years after being declared *excellent*. True many of them like Apple, IBM and Xerox have reinvented themselves and are once more forces to be reckoned with, but look at where they are coming from. Xerox for instance invented the *Xerox* technology and then settled down to business as usual until Canon came along. Xerox became thoroughly complacent and at a point had an advert byline that went … '*we taught the world to copy.*' Who cares? Canon did not care. Sharp did not care. Minolta did not care. So don't praise yourself, just press on with the job of remaining excellent and sustaining your lead.

In June 2007, Samsung, the Korean electronic giant achieved a great milestone in its history – it surpassed Motorola to become the No. 2 top seller of mobile phones world wide. It shipped 37.4 million units relative to 35.5million shipped by Motorola. Guess what, Samsung did not make noise about the feat – as Fortune of September 10, 2007 reported, the company did not even issue a press release. However, this is not where the story ends. Samsung is not satisfied with being No. 2. As the same Fortune reported, at a wireless industry conference earlier this year, telecom chief Gee Sung Choi made it clear he's gunning for the market leader, Nokia, which sold 100 million mobile phones the last quarter. ''*There is no reason we cannot catch up with Nokia"* Choi was quoted as telling the conference. Contrast Samsung with Nigerian companies that go about making noises at every turn and declaring how great they are. The banks are the most voluble in this regard. They go about collecting awards from third rate European publications and local newspapers with dubious credentials that declare them *The Banker of the Year, Fastest Growing, Best Overall* simply because they advertise in these magazines and newspapers. Ironically, none of these publications has ever declared Samsung, the Manufacturer of the Year.

Among Nigerian banks, at least four, amongst them UBA, Intercontinental, Zenith, and Oceanic at a point declared themselves the best and biggest. In the 2009 edition of Bridges we asked "what has size got to do with outstanding customer service? It would appear the bigger the banks become, the worse their service!" As if to answer our rhetorical question, the Central Bank of Nigeria in May 2009 seized Oceanic Bank and Intercontinental Bank for being terminally ill with liabilities exceeding assets and shareholders funds fully depleted. Among banks in Nigeria with satisfactory customer service pedigree was GTBank which today also has subsidiaries in Gambia, Ghana, Liberia and Sierra Leone and the UK. With its shares now also listed on both the Nigerian and London Stock Exchanges, GTB has been blowing its trumpet, and its advert tag line not long ago was '*Internationally quoted, internationally recognized.*' A close observation reveals that the sheen on the GTB's service armour is gradually becoming dim since it altered its business strategy to face the mass market. GTB needs to recalibrate its service strategy too. It took Union Bank 92 years to find itself in the quandry it is today. With barely 20 years of history behind it, GTB is too young to toy with its service pedigree. 'As Brian Pitman, the late Chairman and CEO of the then Lloyds Bank once said: "*It is a myth that biggest is best. It is much more difficult to be the best than it is to be the biggest.*" Brian Pitman went on to assert that only the best can be the "*strongest, and most profitable.*" He hit the nail right on the head by stating unequivocally that the best bank is the one with "*the highest reputation for serving customers and having the highest quality staff.*" Whether you are serving the mass market like GTBank or the corporate market like Zenith, you must find a way to maintain the integrity of your service standard. Wells Fargo Bank is clearly a model in this regard and GTB may wish to move to replicate their strategy than throw up its arms in surrender because it serves a mass market.

According to Kevin Gavaghan, the then Marketing Director, UK Banking, of the then Midland Bank, differentiating in terms of quality customer service prowess is a powerfull competitive advantage for banks. According to him *"successful banks will be those that respond to the paradigm of changing and increasing customer expectation in the best integrated, most stable and responsive way, while maintaining profitability at a level acceptable to the owners of the business."*

As Brian Pitman and Kevin Gavaghan have both sought to emphasize, its quality service and responsiveness to customers' needs that matter, how big you are is not really the issue. Seeing how size was working against GM, Alfred Sloan lamented at the twilight of his reign that due to size GM could never be a leader as the inertia brought about by size was so great that the effort to bring anything new into effect would be *"considered insignificant in comparison with the effort that it takes to put it across."* To turn a supertanker around is never easy and the great Alfred Sloan got it right on target.

Anyone who has been following the news would have heard that on January 21, 2009, Toyota announced it overtook GM as the biggest seller of vehicles worldwide. Toyota sold about 600,000 more than GM in 2008. In acknowledging that fact GM sought to play down the significance of Toyota's feat by saying through their spokeman that size no longer mattered to GM as their focus hence forth was profitability. Ironically, Toyota is far more profitable than GM, which in 2008 went cap-in-hand to Washington D.C., together with Ford and Chrysler, for a whopping $45billion bailout of the US auto industry. As was widely predicted, in early 2009, GM went into Chapter 11 (short for bankruptcy) and got the necessary breather to restructure its operations. In January 2011 it strode out majestically from Chapter 11, a healthier, nimbler and more profitable organization, with its cars now sold all over the world, including Nigeria, where they are giving Toyota a fight for their money. As you pursue size be warned the fate of GM may catch up with you unless you get your service strategy right.

Bridge Twenty Six

DON'T EVER IN YOUR LIFE TELL THE CUSTOMER:

- I don't know

- It's not my job

- I'm on break

- We have closed

- Our computer is down

- My computer is hanging

- There is nothing I can do

- I forgot

- The guy in charge is on vacation

- I'll do it tomorrow

- I'm going for a meeting

- Ask the next guy

- I'm busy

- I wish I can help

- I went to the gents

- I'm in a bad mood

- I have a headache

- I'm feeling sleepy

- My car broke down

- I'm broke

- My wife was admitted in the hospital

- NEPA took light

- I lost my Blackberry

- Our gen broke down

- I was tipsy yesterday

Beware, all the excuses in the world will not guarantee you delighted customers. If anything, they will ensure you remain mediocre, ever looking for excuses why you and your organization cannot deliver quality service. As the Chinese saying goes, *he who wants to do a job looks for the tools, he who does not want looks for excuses.*

Bridge Twenty Seven

CHARGE THE CUSTOMER FULLY FOR YOUR EXCELLENT SERVICE - HE WILL GLADLY PAY!

Companies with reputation for excellent service are profitable not because they charge more but because their costs are always invariably lower. Why? A few reasons: they have lower staff turnover, lower warranty cost, lower inventory cost, lower error rates, lower overall cost of doing business.

Besides lower cost structure, excellent companies can actually charge a price premium for their service and customers will gladly pay. Take Transcorp Hilton, its room rates are consistently priced at a premium of about $200, and yet it has the highest occupancy rates of all hotels in Abuja. Its service may not be comparable to other 5-Star Hotels elsewhere, but be rest assured in the country of the blind, as Chinua Achebe noted in his *Things Fall Apart*, "*the one-eyed man is the king.*" Yet, truly great companies are able to charge premium price for their service and customers have no compunction paying. That's the case with the Dubai based Murj-Al Arab Hotel, the only 7-Star hotel in the world, and the most expensive. That is why Nigeria's *new generation* banks are generally able to charge more than their old generation counterparts.

The fact that excellent companies can charge a premium for their services has been well documented in the PIMS (Profit Impact of Market Strategies) studies led by Robert Buzzell and Bradley Gale. In their seminal study, Buzzel and Gale documented that excellent companies were able to charge 9 per cent higher than the not-so-excellent companies. In the Nigerian aviation industry, Dana Airlines, Air Nigeria, Aero Contractors and Arik Air consistently charge higher than other airlines as their services are perceived, and are indeed better, than those of AES, IRS, and Chachangi. In the long distance passenger bus service, ABC Transport consistently charges higher than other transporters as its service is considered far higher than that of other transporters such as Ekene Dili Chukwu, CHISCO, De Young, to mention a few. In satellite broadcasting Multichoice should be able to charge a premium as they have more variety of services compared to Startimes and HITV. The same rule plays out in all other industries or businesses, whether health care, business schools, consulting, you name it; the best ones are always able to charge higher than the second, third and fourth best. Aim high on quality, charge the customer, he will gladly pay!

Bridge Twenty Eight

TAKE CARE OF THE CUSTOMER AND EVERYTHING ELSE WILL TAKE CARE OF ITSELF

The Bridge take care of the customer and everything else will take care of itself end the strategy section and is the summation of the whole essence of this book. It is all so obvious that giving our all to the customer is the essence of business. Peter Drucker has said *'the sole purpose of business is to create and keep a customer.'* Yet it's so amazing to see businesses, large and small, set up shop and then turn their backs on the customer.

If you live by the tenets of Bridge Twenty Eight, you would have gained the full value for this book because as we have said, it's the embodiment of everything we have said so far. Philip Crosby, probably one of the most passionate preachers of total quality, in reviewing the critical elements required to run a successful organization that could endure forever came to the conclusion in his book, **The Eternally Successful Organization,** that myriad elements are involved but the key is the people. According to Crosby *"if we take care of the customers and the employees, everything else takes care of itself. It is hard to find an organization that both customers and employees regard with continuous affection and appreciation".* Roland M. Fortuna, in the paper **The Quality Imperative**, as published in the book **Total Quality: The Manager's Guide for the 1990s**, stated that there is more to quality than what people say it is when talking in the traditional sense of quality of product and services. According to him the all encompassing definition includes *"improvement in cost position, delivery performance, time taken to get products unto the market, and responsiveness to changes in the market-place."*

Every thing to do with quality starts and ends with customer. How can we serve him better? How can we get the product to her faster? How can we present him the product with the latest innovation? How can we get the product to her at the best price" As Roland M. Fortuna puts it, *"It is a bottom line issue that addresses the very roots of a business and it requires a change of thinking from the top of the organization to the bottom."* Stew Leonard's, a company we have cited as one of our prime examples throughout this book, is the very epitome of quality in the grocery business. The company lives and breaths quality and focuses all its decisions on the customer, not profit, not size. The bedrock of the company's policy is the believe that the customer is always right. As its website explains, the company founded in 1969 as a small dairy store with seven employees is today not only the world's largest, but one of the most renowned. The accolades it has won, which include "largest sales per square foot for a single grocery store: $115million in sales, $3,470 per square foot" (1992 Guinness Book of World Records), "Best Supermarket in New England (Yankee Magazine, 2005)' "100 Best Companies to Work For" (Fortune 2008), to mention just a few are testimonies to the company's renown. What has made Stew Leonard's so outstanding? Care for the customer. Stew Leonards has two Rules. Rule #1: The Customer Is Always Right. Rule #2: If the Customer Is Ever Wrong, Refer to Rule #1! With its legendary service do you still wonder how Stew Leonard got into The Guinness Book of World Records?

PART 2

PROMOTING SERVICE ZEALOTRY

Bridge Twenty Nine

DO *WHATEVER* IT TAKES TO SATISFY THE CUSTOMER

The key words here are *whatever it takes*. Doing whatever it takes to satisfy the customer can be a difficult bridge to cross in the journey to delivering what Tom Peters calls *WOW! Se*rvice. Bridge twenty nine is a way of thinking and has to be ingrained in the mindset of every staff of the firm. What Bridge twenty nine does is that it helps create the mental attitude that says, look, we are here for the customer. This mental conditioning is very important for it enables people in the company see everything from what Peter Drucker calls 'the outside-in' perspective: from the point of view of the customer. Staff in this mental mode can do wonders. To make it happen the management, the board of directors inclusive, must create the enabling environment that says focusing on the customer is okay. Management must empower people with information and eliminate all bureaucratic bottlenecks to enable people bend backwards to satisfy the customer.

In the book **The Pursuit of WOW!** Tom Peters did what he said had previously not been done in publishing history by having the pictures of his service heroes and heroines printed in the book. One of such pictures was that of Virginia Azuela, the housekeeper of the 54th floor of the Ritz Carlton in San Francisco. The beef in the story was that Ms. Azuela had authority to spend up to $2,000 ($2,000 in 1994 money) to fix any customer's problem without further sign off from above. Ms Azuela is indirectly the CEO of the 54th floor of Ritz Carlton. That is the stuff bridge twenty nine is made of. Any wonder the Ritz Carlton was the first service company to win the coveted Malcolm Baldridge National Award for Quality.

Contrast Ritz Carlton with Nigerian government ministers that don't have authority to spend a dime without clearance from the Accountant General of the Federation, the Auditor General of the Federation, the Due Process Office, and the Presidency.

Any wonder National Electric Power Authority (NEPA) now Power Holding Company of Nigeria (PHCN) cannot give light, Nigeria Telecoms (NITEL) cannot give dialing tone, NIPOST cannot deliver letters and roads nationwide are a throwback to the age of the caveman. You may say the conditions are different. I disagree. Service is service and it matters little whether it's rendered by a Ministry of Education, a Ministry of Works, an Exxon Mobil, a MR BIGGS or the mom and pop corner shop, government or private sector. The Nigerian government after a recent executive cabinet meeting announced that it was removing all spending limitations from its ministers and ministers can go ahead and spend to get things done. In announcing the feat, the then Minister of Information and Communication, Prof. Dora Akunyili, stated there was however a caveat to prevent abuse: the blank check was only to be used in case of "emergencies" or "direct procurement from manufacturers." With the caveat, your guess whether any road would be tarred this year is as good as mine.

If you think working in a government ministry or agency is a catastrophic impediment to delivering excellent service you are making a huge mistake, as the following story by Mark Sanborn illustrates. In his book **The Fred Factor: How Passion in Your Work and Life Can Turn the Ordinary into the Extraordinary**, Mark Sanborn gives a captivating account of Fred Shea, a staff of U.S. Postal Service, who was responsible for delivering postal mails in the Denver area called Washington Park. "Let's face it", John Maxwell, the author of **The 21 Irrefutable Laws of Leadership**, wrote in the foreword of The Fred Factor, *"if a guy named Fred, who has a less-than glamorous job working for the U.S. Postal Service, can serve his customers with exceptional service and commitment, what opportunities wait you and me to help others and, in the process, achieve deeper personal satisfaction".* Fred's story began when Mark Sanborn, a professional speaker relocated to Denver. Mark recounted that Fred came to introduce himself and get acquainted, and welcome him to the area. Having not encountered a postal man that was so proud and passionate about his job, Mark was naturally astounded. On learning that Mark was a professional speaker that travelled quite frequently, Fred quickly suggested that in that case he would hold Mark's mails until he was sure Mark was home before delivering them. Somewhat taken aback, Mark not wanting to inconvenience the guy indicated that it was really not necessary, that Fred should just drop the mails in the mail box. Fred would not take any of that. He informed Mark that he could become a victim of burglary as mails building up in a box could signal to burglars that the house occupant was not home. To break the deadlock, Fred suggested that he would put mails in the box so long as it would lock, and put the rest between the front screen door and the main door so long as the place was not congested with mails. Any mail that could not fit in, Fred suggested he would hold them until Mark was back. That way no one would notice the mails. Mark concluded *"I started using my experiences with Fred as illustrations in speeches and seminars that I presented across the United States."* No matter the industry they came from, everybody wanted to hear about Fred, the author said.

What an amazing story! Fred has gone on to inspire thousands of people all over the US, including teachers, nurses, ambulance drivers, and the like. I could not help but reflect deeply after I first read the highly inspirational book. The more I reflected, the less I could pin point one redeeming attribute in the Nigerian public service worker. Water board never has water for drinking, fire service never has water to fight fire, NIPOST never delivers letter on schedule, NITEL's telephone lines never work, PHCN never has light! What a depressing and drab customer service landscape!!

My personal experience with NIPOST (Nigeria's Postal Service) would make you want to throw up. On a trip to Canada in August 2008 to attend Toastmasters International Annual Convention at Calgary I'd ordered some CDs from a company called Maximum Advantage. I was promised four weeks lead time before delivery but by October I'd still not reveived the CDs so I sent email to Paul Endress the CEO, who personally took my order. There was a flurry of emails with Linda Ebersole, the Accounting and Operations Director, who confirmed the order was shipped on August 18, 2008 by US AIR MAIL Priority. She even quoted US Customs number used as CP654333524US. With such detail it was quite obvious the parcel had been shipped. So where was it? I agreed with Linda that she would check the US end while I checked the Nigeria end, with the understanding that if the parcel was not found, a replacement would be shipped within days. In one of her emails while the search was on, Linda wrote *''I will go to the post office here and see about attempts to start a trace of this package using the customs code. Please keep me apprised via email as we will resolve this problem in whatever manner you wish."* Right on target: Do *whatever* it takes to satisfy the customer.

To cut a long story short, when my wife furtitously stopped by at Agege Post Office, the parcel was found gathering dust. The lady on duty casually said "the owner had not come for it". No apology was tendered. NIPOST had received the parcel on 19 August and no one bothered to send the addressee a notice. I got the parcel on 17 October

2008, some 61 days after it was posted. It was with NIPOST for 58 days gathering dust. What a shame! Also, contrast this experience with the one I had with The Chartered Institute of Bankers, London. Now known as Institute of Financial Services, as a student member in the 1980s, I'd ordered a set of books for a whopping cost of £120 (a small fortune for me then) to aid my exam preparation. The books were never delivered. The best *IFS* did was to direct me to check "your local post office," with a stiff British upper lip. They didn't say *"we will resolve this problem in whatever manner you wish"*, as Maximum Advantage did

Now is the situation any different in the private sector? Talk of the small company. How many times do you walk into an office and you see hung on the wall exhortations such as *'the customer is the king'*, *'you ask, we deliver'* and such like. And you see the company's beautifully made brochure at the reception and you ask the beautiful girl there can I have that brochure, and she looks into your eyes, smiles and then tells you no. And you ask why not and she informs you the MD said no one should take it away because it is for the reception, it's company property. You drag on till eternity and she just smiles but does not budge. Sounds familiar? Now go a step further, call a more senior officer and ask for the same brochure, and he tells you, why not? But why didn't the smiling girl at the reception know the customer could have the brochure if she requested? The simple reason may be that they don't just give it away. The less obvious reason is the lack of empowerment to do *whatever* it takes to satisfy the customer because she lacks the mental attitude and conditioning. In short, the company has not been sold to the idea of customer orientation in words and deeds. Bridge twenty nine is easier said than done. Bridge twenty nine does not mean giving away your company's products and services free. In fact, the customer does not expect you to do that. She however expects you to treat her with dignity, with respect. In short to show that you care, and that you understand her values.

I remember visiting Spectrum Books, the big publishers in Ibadan on October 8, 1998 while thinking about writing this book. When I got there it was raining and nobody offered me an umbrella. The people at the gate checked my identity and gave me the visitors' notebook to complete and bade me good luck as I braced the rain, from the gate-house to the main office, some twenty meters away. Is umbrella important during a rain storm? Should a company have one for its customers and visitors? What is the role of the gate people in welcoming visitors to the company? If you were at your home and saw a visitor under the rain, wouldn't you rush out to meet her with an umbrella? So what is different?

I was tickled and thrilled when I read in the March 2010 edition of T + D Magazine that if you go to Chic-fil-A when it is rainning somebody will run and meet you with an umbrella. Dan T. Cathy, Chick-fil-A CEO talked about that with pride. Most Nigerian companies, especially banks, do the umbrella thing but there is no consistency. Sometimes it is just a favour from the gateman or securityman and not closely monitored as an integral part of the service strategy. When a company and its people develop the *Do Whatever It Takes To Satisfy The Customer* mentality, things start to happen. People start seeing little things like rain as important, the umbrella becomes important, answering mails become important, being courteous becomes important, being polite on the phone becomes important, everything becomes important, the customer becomes important, not just in the printed mission statement hanging on the wall or in the annual report. The customer becomes the center of the company's universe. Bridge twenty nine must be ingrained in the hearts and minds of staff of the company as an integral part of the service experience otherwise staff are going to be lackadaisical about it as I witnessed at one of the Protea Hotels in Lagos, on February 14, 2011, St. Valentine's Day. There was a downpour and guests were soaked and there was no umbrella in sight.

Bridge Thirty

PUT THE CUSTOMER FIRST

Put the customer first means exactly what it says. Without the customer, there is no business. Trite you would say. Is this a new idea? No it is not. So, why don't 99.9999% of businesses put the customer first? You would think since every business sets up to provide a service to a customer, every business would *put the customer first*. They don't! In most organizations the employees put their directors first; in government ministries they put the ministers first; in small sole-proprietorships, the staff put the founder first. They hold the car door for the big shots when they alight their limo, they call them sir, they scramble to hold their brief case heavy or not, they laugh at their every dry joke! Yet these same employees would not help their customer if she had a flat tire in their premises! You would need to beg and be willing to part with a big tip.

Put the customer first is best illustrated with the spectacular come back of British Airways. Before 1980, British Airways was like the bankrupt Nigeria Airways. Despite British Airways' motto, *to fly, to serve*, its airplanes flew but the airline never served. At that time, people referred to the acronym, BA, as '*Bloody Awful.*' British Airways lost business to British Caledonian and the upstart Virgin Atlantic and at a point the question was not whether it would go belly up, but when. All that changed in 1981 when Sir John King, later Lord King was appointed chairman of BA, and together with Sir Collin Marshall, whom he appointed as CEO of BA in 1983, launched a series of campaigns to make BA staff more customer focused. One of these campaigns was called *Putting People First.* The campaign involved everybody at BA - the pilots, cabin crew, ground crew, engineers, sales staff, ticketing agents, everybody. This programme focused on the flying passengers, the external customers. The message was simple: the customer comes first. The effect was 180 degrees turn around in orientation, attitude, and reasoning. Example, engineers at BA that used to think only about radar and aircraft came to understand everything they did was done because of the customer. Everybody grappled single mindedly with the one thing that matters: the customer. The whole campaign which revolved around the theme the "World's

Favorite Airline" aimed at making BA the 'best and most successful airline in the world'. Within 10 years of deliberately focusing on customer service British Airways became indeed the *World's Favorite Airline* winning the Business Traveler Airline of the Year Award for four consecutive years (1990, 1991, 1992 and 1993) and the Air Transport World magazine's 'Airline of the Year' Award three years in a row (1991, 1992 and 1993).

Contrast that with the defunct Nigeria Airways. People in Nigeria fancifully referred to it as the national carrier. As at October 1998, the airline had only one aircraft. Do you know any other airline in the world that has only one aircraft? Do you wonder why Nigeria Airways is no more? I will tell you. The airline had no customers before dying unsung. It died without customers because in 1992, the Nigerian government deregulated the airline industry and Nigeria Airways found itself panting for breath. Private airlines such as ADC, Bellview, Okada, Oriental, Kabo invaded the industry and overnight Nigeria Airways lost all its customers. All but one of these airlines have now crashed out of business, but not for lack of customers.

Nigeria Airways had not always been the way it was before it crashed out. In 1962 when it was founded, it had six aircrafts and by 1975 it had 27. But do you know what the airline did? It forgot about customer, and instead, government interference and internal politics became the order of the day. The government-appointed directors knew nothing about the airline business. Flights were never on schedule. To enter a Nigeria Airways plane, you had to race through the tarmac. Tickets were sold by touts. And to get a boarding pass you had to know a minister, the company's MD, an employee or a tout. The airline could not guarantee passengers' luggage. 'Airport rats' saw to that. Now, you can see why Nigeria airways died. Between 1962 and 1992, a period of 30 solid uninterrupted years, passengers had no choice but fly Nigeria Airways, however, when the airline industry was suddenly deregulated by the General Ibrahim Babangida Administration in 1992, passengers suddenly found that they had a choice, and Nigeria Airways paid the inevitable price. You toy with customers at your own peril! Interestingly, between the period the first signs of distress set-in, around the end of 1992, and the time the airline finally collapsed, 10 years later in 2002, it had over six CEOs, an average of about one every one and half years, and none took the bold, you would say, decisive steps that Colin Marshall took to bring British Airways back from the brink of disaster. Two airlines, similar problems, different outcomes! One survived by putting customers first, the other died as it knew little about the customer.

The market place is unforgiving in exacting punishment on those companies that toy with the customer.

On 6 October 1998 I went to Ibadan to attend a seminar at D'Rovans Hotel and in between sessions, I toured some of the beautiful shops doted within the hotel. One shop had the most attraction so I spent more time there. What did I find? The shop attendant was busy dusting, arranging and rearranging items in the shop. I stood there for close to three minutes and she did not even acknowledge my presence. In short I was ignored. I decided to put the hapless girl through my usual twenty seconds training course on customer service when she finished her chores of rearranging items in the shop. I asked her, what was more important, welcoming this man (pointing to myself) to your shop or doing what you were doing? You know what she said? She said 'I didn't know that you wanted to buy something'. I always count how many seconds it takes whoever I meet to acknowledge that I am somebody whenever I enter a place, whether it's the customer service area of a bank, a hospital, a mom-and-pop shop or the minister's office. Nine out of ten times, you don't get the attention you deserve. Most often than not, the 'girl-in-charge' is on the cell phone, or busy with the computer, and the like. In Nigeria, most businesspeople hire expensive locations, stock their shops with expensive items and hand over the shops to their illiterate relatives to run for them with disastrous consequences.

Bridge Thirty One

LOVE THE CUSTOMER

What do you do for the person you love? You kiss her on the cheek? You buy her expensive gifts? Wrong! First, you tell her I love you! Next you do things that show you care. You put your lover's interest above yours. You give more than you expect to receive. When you do all these, chances are the person will come to appreciate you, will honor your actions and will admire everything else you are trying to do. It is after all these that kissing the cheek becomes meaningful. Bridge thirty one, *love the customer,* is reflected in everything we do in our relationship with the customer. If you do not love the customer, if you are merely pretending, the customer will sooner than later find out. As the saying goes, the most difficult thing to give is kindness (change that to love), it is always returned.

I believe loving the customer has to do with having deep respect for the customer. The truth is, you cannot love someone you don't respect. Now, can you respect someone you do not have empathy for? Empathy! Respect!! Love!!! Empathy is putting *yourself* in the other persons shoes. If you empathize with the customer, if you respect the customer, if you love the customer, why should you in this day and age carry warning signs in your parking lot that read "vehicles parked at owner's risk"! What you are indirectly telling the customer is, we don't care about you, we don't care whether you come here or not, in fact we don't know you even exist. Let me ask, do we have such warning signs at our homes? If we don't have warnings that say vehicles parked at owner's risk at our homes, why should our offices be different? At any rate if you have such a warning at your home, let me tell you straight away, you are deeply wrong. Soon you will lose all your friends, and they won't tell you why they stopped coming to your house.

Hotels go a step further to drive away customers and potential customers alike. In addition to having *vehicles parked at owner's risk* signposts, in all but the best hotels, you see boldly written statements that read "the hotel will not accept liability for valuables not left in the custody of the duty manager". What they are telling you indirectly is, look, we cannot vouch for the honesty and integrity of our room keepers. If you keep your money in your room while staying with us, our workers may steal your money, so keep the money with the duty manager to avoid embarrassing us and yourself. When a friend comes visiting us and staying over night, we go all out to make the friend comfortable and in most parts of Africa, we surrender to the visitor the best bed in the house. The hotel guest on the other hand is strictly warned to leave her money and other valuable items with the duty manager! We don't tell our visitors that. We assure her she will be safe, her money will be safe, her trinkets will be safe, and everything will be safe. Should your wayward child decide to play pranks with your friend's money, you don't go to the police (at least not in Nigeria) or tell your friend he was stupid to have kept money in the guest room. You apologize deeply and tell your friend not to mention it to any other person. You refund the stolen money and invite your friend to visit again.

Bridge Thirty One, *Love the Customer* means we assume full responsibility for the welfare and wellbeing of the customer whenever he comes around to do business with us. Empathy means putting ourselves in the other person's shoe. The second most important law of God says we should love our neighbors as we love ourselves, which broadly translates to doing unto others what we would like done unto us, the *golden rule*. When a customer comes to do business with us, maybe he is coming to withdraw money from her bank account in our bank, or coming to spend the weekend in our hotel with his family, are we showing love by telling her the vehicle will not be safe in our premises, that he is parking the vehicle at her own risk, that if she does not count the money in the presence of a bank teller, we would not believe her if she says there was a shortage? How then do we expect her to enjoy her stay with us or value our bank if she cannot take her mind off her car or trust our tellers? If you think this is too difficult or impossible to do, remember L.L. Bean Golden Rule, which we talked about in Bridge Twelve: Guarantee Your Customers' Satisfaction.

To say that L.L. Bean thought and practiced love for the customer as far back as 1912 is instructive. You must unconditionally guarantee the safety of your customer and her property while she is in your premises otherwise, why on earth should she do business with you? The customer, whether an account holder in a bank, a hotel guest, a school student, a restaurant patron, a church member, you name it, does not pitch her tent with you simply because you have the most elegant building in town, which cost many millions of dollars to build or because you have the best technology money can buy. She comes there because you love the most, your tellers count the best, your food tastes the most delicious, your teachers teach the most, your preaching makes the best sense, your hotel is the safest, your police officers are the most firm but friendly, I can go on and on and on. If you cannot unconditionally guarantee any of these things, I can unconditionally guarantee that you will fail. When will you fail? I don't know but you will fail all the same. Ask Nigeria Airways!

Bridge Thirty Two

HAVE REAL PASSION FOR THE CUSTOMER

The Bridge **Have Real Passion For The Customer** means you become a quality customer service fanatic, you become obsessed with quality management, you display individual and collective zealotry, you do things unthinkable that others can only imagine (like instant refund when a bank customer reports a shortage), you provide heroic service (like dashing across a railway line to snatch a stray child moments before she's crushed by a bullet train hurtling down the line at 350 km/hr). It means you're willing to go the second, third, hundredth mile for the customer. The inspirational sequel to **In Search of Excellence** was appropriately titled **A Passion For Excellence**. The book written by Tom Peters and Nancy Austin is replete with endless anecdotes, stories, folklores and sagas of how the most innovative and best companies such as Perdew Farm, Sewell Village Cadillac, Stew Leonard's, L. L. Bean, Ritz Carlton, etc. display unbelievable passion for the customer.

A survey in 1992 of service employees by Inset Systems Coy of Brookfield, Connecticut, concerning what *'quality'* means in terms of job performance yielded among other responses this one, *"giving your all and going all out to die for the customer".* That is what I call passion! Tom Peters and Robert Waterman Jr.'s **In Search of Excellence: Lessons from America's Best-Run Companies**, the book described by Warner Books as the best selling business book of all time, brought the whole idea of quality service down to earth, to the language that could be understood by all, described *'twelve attributes'* or traits of the *'quality revolution'.* The first two attributes are "*management obsession with quality*" and "*passionate systems*". As the authors pointed out, *''management obsession for quality stresses the importance of practical action to back up the emotional commitment to quality'', e.g. 'never walking past shoddy goods.'* Passionate systems, the authors stated, are important in the pursuit of quality, for failure can be brought about by *'passion without system, or system without passion.'*

The book described graphic instances where workers displayed passion and sometimes heroism in their drive to deliver outstanding service. I have three favorites. One was about the Honda worker who, *"on his way home each evening, straightens up windshield wiper blades on all the Hondas he passes. He just can't stand to see a flaw in a Honda."* Then there was the car salesman Joe Girard. He sold more new cars and trucks, each year, for eleven years running, than any other human being. In a typical year, Peters said, *"Joe sold more than twice as many units as whoever was in second place"*. What is Joe's magic? As the authors told the story, *"every month throughout the year Joe's customers get a letter from him. It arrives in a plain envelop, always a different size or color. And they open it up and the front of it reads, 'I LIKE YOU'."* Joe Girard sent cards to his customers without tiring. Any wonder, Joe Girard ended up in the Guinness Book of World Records as the greatest car salesman of all time. Then there is the Frito-Lay's 10,000-person sales force that braved rain, snow, sleet and mud to restock their customers' stores with potato chips to uphold the *"99.5 percent service level"*. These are the stuffs passion is made of.

Now contrast the above stories with the experience you will generally get from the average Nigerian worker. There is the PHCN worker who will not bother to read your electricity meter but will send you a bill at the end of the month; there is the NITEL worker who will use your telephone line to make international calls and debit the bill to your account; there is the potatoes farmer who will use a false bottom to sell you potatoes; and there is the boutique operator who will sell you second hand clothes as new ones, the list is endless. No doubt, most of these examples amount to fraud but they also underscore a crass devil-may-care attitude to the customer. Passion is not something you go to Harvard Business School to learn. It is not rocket science that requires extraordinary IQ. As we can see in the Honda, Frito Lay and Joe Girard examples it's about thinking deep about what is important. It's about the focus of the company. It's about culture. It's about people selection.

The first step towards passion is selecting the right people as Jack Welch, the legendary former CEO of GE and one of the world's most acclaimed business leaders of the current generation, emphasized in his superb book, **Winning**. *"Hiring great people is brutally hard"* Jack avowed, *'and yet nothing matters more in winning than getting the right people on the field."* As Jack Welch implied all the strategic plans, super computers are worthless if you don't have the right men and women in place. Management expert and co-author of **The One Minute Manager**, Ken

Blanchard, recounts in his latest Book, **The Secret**, co-authored with Mark Miller, former Vice President, Training and Development, Chick-fil-A, Inc., that Peter Drucker, the management and leadership guru that literally founded the management body of knowledge as we know it today, was asked, '*What is the most important decision an executive makes*?' He responded, '*Who does what*?' Getting the right people in the right jobs is the most important job of the leader, it cannot be delegated as we earlier pointed out. To manage people well, Jack Welch postulates the following company-wide practices, amongst others, '*Elevate HR to a position of power and primacy in the organization, and make sure HR people have the special qualities to help managers build leaders and careers.*" Welch compared or said the best HR people came across as "*pastors and parents*" rolled into one.

Contrast the above prescription with the levity with which Nigerian CEOs, especially in the banking sector, treat HR matters. Staff turnover in fact is encouraged. I remember whilst still a staff of one of the top banks pointing out to my then director that it appeared to me that our staff turnover was too high and therefore unsustainable in the long run. She stunned me by saying I shouldn't worry that it was the same in the whole industry. That led me to send a memo to her in which I recommended a 10-point action plan among which was " *Acknowledge that the current level of staff turnover is unsustainable and therefore unacceptable. Take all available remedial action to dissuade staff from leaving. The attitude that we can always get replacements is misinformed.*" I didn't get an acknowledgement.

Nordstrom is one of the best companies in the world where staff display uncommon zeal and passion to ensure no customer leaves a Nordstrom shop unhappy. In highlighting why Nordstrom is so successful, Robert Spector and Patrick D. McCarthy in their **The Nordstrom Way: The Inside Story of America's #1 Customer Service Company**, stated ''*Nordstrom's best sales people will do virtually everything possible to ensure that a shopper leaves the store a satisfied customer*''

Bridge Thirty Three

BE TOTALLY, ABSOLUTELY, COMPLETELY, UNCOMPROMISINGLY CUSTOMER ORIENTED

What is the level of your customer orientation? Ninety nine per cent? Well, that means that if you're like the Power Holding Company of Nigeria (PHCN) with 100m customers, 1m of them are not happy; if you're like Coca Cola with three quarters of the human beings on earth drinking your products, it means 40m of your customers worldwide are not happy, and if you're a small professional services firm just starting out with 10 customers, it means one of those customers is not happy, talk-less of being delighted! It means to one customer your service stinks. You might even be surprised to learn that all your customers are not satisfied and are just waiting for an alternative service provider to come along for them to dump you. Good riddance at last to *bad rubbish* they'd exclaim as they ditch you! Stinking service is like an iceberg, most of the time it's only the tip that you see while the mass of it is buried deep in the water

The Bridge, be totally, absolutely, completely, uncompromisingly customer oriented is a subset of the Bridge have passion for the customer. Have passion for the customer is concerned with focus on service zealotry at the individual staff level (the MD or supervisor will not be there when the rude staff shocks the customer with service that is 1 on a scale of 10), while the Bridge be totally, absolutely, completely, uncompromisingly customer oriented focuses on service zealotry at the organization-wide level. Organization-wide focus on quality is concerned with the structures, systems, processes put in place by management (who else?) to ensure the organization is organically and dynamically orientated towards the customer. The Bridge is concerned with organizational culture that says, we will go out as a team and *die* for the customer; it is concerned with a culture that empowers the staff to do whatever it takes to satisfy the customer; it is concerned with a culture that says *we will stand by you* if you make a mistake in the process of going all out to serve the customer. In delivering outstanding customer service you can't tell the staff to show obsession for the customer and punish him when he commits a mistake in the process of doing just that.

Robert Galvin tells the story that when Motorola started its quality programme a staff took an action that cost the company $10,000 and the staff was invited to the chairman's office for a chat. Not knowing what to expect, the staff asked when he got to the Chairman's office, "You're going to sack me, ain't it?" You know what Galvin told the guy? He told him, 'you have just made us $10,000 wiser' and he promoted the guy. Now that is another name for leadership.

In 1986, after a rigorous market and other surveys that showed that customers preferred the *new* coke, Coca Cola rolled out the new product in the US amid fanfare. Within hours of the rollout, Coca Cola received 10,000 calls from all over the country denouncing *new* coke. Eventually, Coca Cola was compelled to abandon *new* coke and return to the classic formula. Now if Coca Cola had said, hey, we spent $1,000,000.00 for the research for new coke and the result confirms the new formula is smoother than the old formula. Take new coke or leave it, after all we are the *#1* soft drink company in the world, it would have lost. You see the customer is always right and Coke knows it.

Being uncompromisingly customer oriented is about empowerment and more. It's about a *culture of excellence.* This culture must be pervasive. Management must walk-the-talk and do everything to show the staff that posters and batches with *Q* inscribed in the center are not just rhetoric and showmanship. If you don't stand by your staff when they goof, they will come to believe that management is not to be trusted. And your effort will fail. In Japanese auto manufacturing plants, you have switches directly in front of all assembly line workers and any assembly worker can pull the switch to stop the assembly line if he notices an error or fault in the line. The stoppage enables the fault to be corrected before the line is restarted. This practice allows upstream and ongoing prevention, meaning faulty goods are not passed from one stage of the manufacturing process to another. Unless a company is *Totally, Absolutely, Completely and Uncompromisingly Customer Oriented*, it will not give frontline assembly workers such powers. Don't forget here we are talking about focus on both the internal and external customers.

Contrast the Japanese attitude with the attitude at Ford Motor Company as represented in the story told by David T. Kearns and David A. Nadler in their excellent book **Prophets in the Dark: How Xerox Reinvented Itself and Beat Back the Japanese**. The story is instructive and reinforces the fact that market rewards those that dare to focus on the customer! Kearns and Nadler related the story that the Japanese car makers started penetrating the US market from the West Cost, around Carlifornia. While the top brass at Ford's headquarters at Dearborn, Michigan, thought the Japanese had nothing to offer, one of Ford's West Coast Managers, Pipp, realised the potential threat of the Japanese invasion. To convince his top management he invited some senior people to his plant to take a close look at how well made the cars and trucks were. Pipp had in fact bought a Toyota truck and disassembled it to the last bolt and reassembled it and to his amazement, the truck was in engineering terms made of "snap-fit" parts. To really convince himself, he tried it a second time and was astounded that he never required a rubber mallet to put any part together unlike Ford's trucks. The truck was indeed made 100% of snap-fit parts. An engineering revolution. Toyota was making its parts to more exacting standard than Ford was making theirs. It was this discovery that prompted Pipp to invite senior management to take a look and perhaps have a rethink on the threat the Japanese posed. When they finally came what they saw left them speechless. The authors say *"Everyone was very quiet, until the division general manager cleared his throat and remarked: 'The customer will never notice.'"* The general manager having said so, everyone else of course concurred and they all left the place satisfied. How sad! Today we all know better. The customer did in fact noticed and and as the saying goes, the rest is now history.

From 0% global market share in automobiles in 1959, the Japanese today control close to 40% global market share in automobiles and their global share keeps increasing by the day. For the first time Toyota surpassed General Motors as the world's largest maker of automobiles in 2007 (Fortune May 2007). How different the story would have been if Ford's management had listened way back in the 70s. How different the story would have been if GM's management had cared about quality and the customer. W. Edwards Deming, the father of *Quality* as we have come to know it today, emphasized time and again that top management holds the key to quality. In one of his very last articles, printed in the **Executive Excellence Magazine**, Deming, as in the past, stressed, *"quality is made in the boardroom"*. Deming, as we earlier noted cited the case of a bank, and stressed that a bank may fail despite having excellent operations. Reviewing suggestions and recommendations most companies make for improving quality, such as automation, incentive pay, rankings, staff motivation, merit systems and the like Deming remarked, "*The fallacies are obvious – every one of them focuses on systems, not the customer!*"

In a lecture to undergraduates at Utah State University in 1983 Deming admonished the students that a company run on financial figures alone must fail because, as he put it, the most important figures are '*unknown or unknowable*'. Only fanatical focus on people can guarantee survival. It is said that while Michelangelo was painting in his late 70s one of his greatest works, the Sistine Chapel, and going blind as the paint was dripping into his eyes as he had to lie on his back, friends and family members urged the septuagenerian to leave out some of the hidden corners for as they put it "*no one would see.*" Michelangelo retorted reportedly *"God will see."*

Bridge Thirty Four

LET THE CUSTOMER KNOW THAT YOU CARE

Scanning the quality literature I was amazed to discover that the majority of the most powerful concepts on quality start with 'C'. Others may have their own list, but here is mine: *Communication, Cooperation, Coordination, Conviction, Constancy, Consistency, Customer, Change, Concentration, Commitment, Consideration, Convention, and Challenge.* Now let's add *Care*.

Others have written about the other Cs, so let's look at *CARE.* How do you show the customer that you care? You buy flowers for her? Visit her on her birthday? Tell her 'I care.' All those have a role to play but let me relate a story as told by Laurie Beth Jones in **Jesus CEO**. Now, this is an emotional story. A truly life and death story that could have ended in tragedy but for the prescient mind of an angel of outstanding service. I like this story because it encapsulates the whole essence of the care dimension of excellence. Laurie was talking about Art Huskey, an estate agent in San Diego. The story recounts an episode where Art, having not heard for a while from an elderly couple (customers) he'd sold a house decided to pay them a surprise visit. Art found the elderly couple utterly dehydrated and rushed them to hospital and took care of them until they were discharged. Even after they were discharged from hospital Art brought them hot chicken soup for weeks not minding the cost. It turned out the elderly couple had been struck by a severe cold, which was so acute they could not even make a phone call to any one to ask for help. Art in short saved this couple's lives. Laurie Beth Jone, the author, who said she learnt of the story from her mum commented *"It seems every time I meet someone who knows Art, he has a similar story to tell."* Art Huskey according to the author *"outsells all other estate agents by five to one where ever he goes."* Tom Peters preaches *'staying close'* to the customer. Art Huskey would not have saved this elderly couple if he had not 'stayed close.' Art may lose money directly by his acts of kindness but he gets hundreds of referrals from his grateful customers.

Horst Schulze, president and COO of The Ritz-Carlton Hotel Company, the 1992 winner of the Malcolm Baldridge National Quality Award, in writing about the need to deliver service with care and sincerity, painted the following hypothetical service situation. Assuming you go to a bank and request to change a ten dollar bill and the teller greets you warmly and goes ahead and give you your correct change, then he has done his job. But he says it shouldn't stop there. The teller should also show care. Horst Schulze concluded by saying that the caring aspect comes on top of the product. *"The product, is giving correct change. But if the teller then adds, 'Sir, I'm happy to give you the change, and please have a wonderful day,' then he has served me."* By giving the correct change, and displaying enthusiasm and courtesy in the process and wishing the customer well, Schulze reasoned, the teller is *"rendering both quality and service."* Contrast the painted scenario with your typical daily experience, be it in the banking halls of our megabanks, a commuter bus and the like. More often that not, the bank teller will not only just push your bundles of cash to you, he will strive to short pay you (though, in fact, this is becoming rarer), the bus conductor will not only be rude, he'll never have change for you, the lady answering the phone at the other end will not only be inattentive, she will ask you to hold on for her to conclude her conversation with her friends, all actions that shout out loud, 'I don't care'.

Care is the most powerful four-letter word in quality service. Sometimes it requires hard work, but more often than that, all that's required is a simple 'welcome sir', 'is there any other thing we can do to help you' and the like. What is necessary to note is that there is a gulf of difference between fact and perception, and as we have constantly emphasized over and over again in this book, perception is more powerful than facts. Show the customer that you care in words and in deed.

Bridge Thirty Five

TELL HEROIC STORIES ABOUT EXCELLENT CUSTOMER SERVICE

Heroic stories are true tales of incredible customer service. Heroic service is service performed with messianic zeal well above and beyond the call of duty. As Robert Spector and Patrick D. McCarthy elaborated on their widely acclaimed *The Nordstrom Way,* "the purpose of heroics is to give people a standard to aspire to - and even surpass." In every organization there are silent miracle workers doing wonderful things for customers. Let your people bring these stories to your attention, verify them independently and then publish them for everybody to hear. Let people know outstanding service will be recognized and rewarded. However, as much as possible avoid monetary reward. You can't pay serious minded people enough. Giving money out can even be a disincentive to excel. Credit your people's emotional bank accounts instead. As the CEO, stop by each recipient's desk and say a simple thank you. Such symbolic gesture performs wonders in people's minds and how they feel.

Which better avenues and channels to tell these stories than your in-house magazines? Fill your magazine with heroic stories about customer service and the heroes. In most companies, their magazine is reserved for the CEO. Ninety percent of the features will be about the CEO - the last paper he delivered at the local chapter conference of the marketing association, his latest award as the most philanthropic individual from his village, picture of him shaking hands with the sultan or praying in the local mosque next to the state governor. What a wasted opportunity. For all intents and purposes this sort of magazine serves no useful purpose other than massaging the ego of the CEO. Check out these CEOs and you will find that they have nothing to offer.

Devoting at least 80% of your in-house magazine space to heroic stories about customer service will add vim to your service culture. Let the stories be really ennobling, inspiring and aspiring. I became challenged to set very high service standard for myself when I first read about the incredible service culture of staff of Frito Lay in **In Search of Excellence**. Such is the power of 'heroics'. It's amazing the motivational impact heroic stories can have on service psyche of individuals that are truly self motivated. As late Sam Walton, the founder of Wal-Mart Stores espoused under Rule 3: in his Ten Rules That Worked For Me, staff should be motivated on a daily basis. He clearly stated that cash and share ownership was not enough. He espoused constant cross pollination, requesting staff to switch jobs, setting high standards and keeping score. He concluded by saying *"Keep everybody guessing as to what your next trick is going to be. Don't become too predictable."* From my personal experience nothing encourages healthy competition more than stories of heroic service.

On January 16, 2009 a crippled US Airways Airbus A320 with 150 passengers and five crewmen on board, piloted by Chesley Sullenberger, spectacularly crash landed on the icy New York's Hudson River and all on board were successfully evacuated. President Obama (then President-elect) according to Agence France Presse praised Sullenberger for the "heroic and graceful job in landing the damaged aircraft." For the rest of US Airways' history, this heroic must be woven into the very fabric of the company, recounted and told to every pilot and crew. Don't be surpised if tomorrow US Airways comes up with an advert with a tag line ~ trust our heroism – with the Hudson River as the backdrop.

Bridge Thirty Six

REWARD PEOPLE WHO GO ALL OUT TO *DIE* FOR THE CUSTOMER

They are one in a million. Unassuming, they go about their work with messianic zeal. They pay great attention to detail and are always looking out how they can help the customer. They will *die* for the customer if need be. To them, smile comes naturally. They love customers. They are service champions.

In world class companies, every staff is a service champion. Even in these centers of excellence, however, some stars shine brighter than the rest. It makes sense to work out a system of recognition for these exceptional people. But this has to be handled with the utmost care. In the first place, the best stars consider it an insult to be singled out for recognition. To them, they are just doing their job and to single them out is to diminish their joy and happiness.

However, on balance, rewarding the best stars is important in many respects. First and foremost, it sends the message that the management is serious about quality. Second, it lets everybody know what's in it for them. Third, reward helps generate fun and enthusiasm.

The nature the reward should take is for the company to decide. Ideally, the reward should be ennobling. As much as possible, cash reward should be avoided as we earlier said, otherwise the whole reward system may be corrupted. McDonalds, arguably the best managed fast-food franchise chain in the world, (though Subway has recently been claiming that accolade), conducts competitions during which their best staff from all over the world compete to select the "best of the best." In the years gone by, IBM, once America's national treasure and before Lou Gerstner took over the helm, sent its best marketing people and their families to vacation in exotic locations, including Hawaii. You can create your own way of rewarding your stars. Make it fun, make it unique. It's the symbolism that matters. But let staff know it's good to be hot for the customer.

Bridge Thirty Seven

EXCEED YOUR CUSTOMER'S EXPECTATION

When you make a phone call, how many times do you expect the phone to ring before someone picks it up at the other end? Is it one, two, or three rings or within 5, 10, or 30 seconds? When your appetite is really fired up and you enter a restaurant, how long do you expect to wait before being served? What of the check out counter in the super market, how long do you expect to wait before they check you out? What of checking in formalities in a hotel? What of a mortgage loan? How long do you have to wait before you get a yes or no answer? And what of admission to say an MBA programme in the average American university? We can go on and on.

Above are representative moments of truth across a variety of businesses. For each of these moments of truth, the customer has his standard expectation. For the majority of customers, the telephone should ring no more than two times; the restaurant customer should be attended to within five seconds but find out what the customer's preference is. The closer you stay to the customer the more you will know what the customer's preference is. You can carry out industry survey to find out what the customers say, but treat this information with a pinch of salt. The more precisely you know the customer, the better able you are to deliver the service to the standard the customer sets. The only standard is the customer's standard and not the industry standard. The industry standard is the status quo and may have emerged in a bygone era.

It is said that Richard Branson took the decision to set up Virgin Atlantic Airlines after spending three days trying to book a flight on North West Airlines from the UK. If all the students frustrated at trying to get admission to Harvard, Stanford, Northwestern, Wharton, Cornel, Columbia, Oxford and all those top rated ivory towers were to set up their universities and business schools, there would have been more business schools than there are students today. But then, where would the Whartons and Harvards of this world be today?

The point of the Bridge, Exceed Your Customer Expectations, is that no matter what the customer says, aim to exceed his expectation by at least one percentage point. In the fight on February 13, 1999 for the WBC welterweight title, Oscar De La Hoya defeated Ghana's Azuma Nelson by a split decision - three versus two. A spilt decision! Oscar became the champ? Azumah? No one remembers him today. In the fight on May 3, 2007, that became the biggest in living history, grossing $120mm, Floyd Mayweather, this time defeated Oscar De La Hoya in a split decision to win the WBC super welterweight world championship at the MGM Grand Garden Arena in Las Vegas. The closing bout of the fight was the most entertaining in recent memory and at the end both boxers were given a standing ovation. Mayweather is the new champ. You can be sure in a few years no one will remember Oscar De La Hoya. In a typical Olympics, the gold medalist for 100m dash always triumph in the magnitude of thousandth of a second (they call it split seconds) on the way to the history books. No one ever remembers the second place winner. Who came next to Carl Lewis in the 100 meters dash, long jump, 100 meters relay and 200 meters at the Los Angeles Olympics in 1984, a meet he won four gold medals to set a games record? You wont remember I assure you except you are the IOC archivist!

Exceed the customer's expectation by a second, a ring, a smile, a thank you, a bouquet of roses, a letter of appreciation, a convenience car, a birthday card and you would have started the journey to what Tom Peters calls *The Pursuit of WOW!* When you consistently exceed the customer's expectation, he becomes what Earl Sasser Jr. calls an 'apostle' to your company, spreading the good news of your legendary service to all and sundry. Nordstrom, arguably one of the best customer service companies in the world, was advertised, until very recently, only by word of mouth by its million of satisfied customer apostles. Marketers call it viral marketing. The type that swept US President, Barack Obama, to the White House. On the other hand, when you dish out mediocre service to customers as standard, the relationship can deteriorate to the point where the customer becomes in the word of Earl Sasser Jr., a *'terrorist'*, *bad mouthing* you for your mediocre service to the ends of the earth. The ultimate in this terrorist scenario is the case where customers band together to take class action suit against a mediocre service provider as it happened against a Canadian dentist many years back. What you can do to exceed the customer's expectation is practically limitless. It only requires a little bit of ingenuity on your part and the willingness and the courage to listen, to experiment and to do what the customer wants, and then going beyond that.

Bridge Thirty Eight

KNOW THAT THE CUSTOMER CAN NEVER BE WRONG

Believe it 100 per cent! It is suggested by some management gurus that sometimes you have to defy the customer as he does not always know what he wants. The customer after all can be very fickle and inconsistent. The purveyors of this theory point to the fact that the video recorder, camcorder, iPod and such revolutionary gadgets were conceived, designed, developed and patented before any customer ever dreamed of them. But don't be deceived.

Take the American auto industry as an extreme example. In the 1970s, the small Japanese cars made their debut in America's highways. Before long, they were everywhere; Americans bought them in record numbers. By the 1980s, the American auto industry was tottering on the brink of bankruptcy. The issue at stake was fuel economy following the quadrupling of oil prices in 1976 as a direct result of the Arab-Israeli 6-day war and the Arab oil embargo. Rather than face this reality, the big three Detroit based car manufacturers G.M, Ford and Chrysler, thought small cars were a passing fad and a matter of nationalism. Who would trade a Cadillac or an Edsel for a Corolla or Mazda they argued? To appeal to customers, adverts such as *Buy America!* became popular. But the customers were not swayed. Rather, customers went out and bought more Japanese cars. Detroit forgot that buying a Japanese car did not necessarily mean the customer was unpatriotic. It simply meant the Customer is *Never Wrong*. The customer always knows what he wants.

Today, the Americans have more or less caught up with the Japanese. How did they do it? By pursuing *quality! Quality* became *Job #1* at Ford. The other car makers followed suit. The battle-ground had changed. And the customers rewarded them to the extent that by 1996, G.M's Taurus became America's best selling car, relegating Honda Acura to second place. No more were customers asked to buy America.

The customer is *Never Wrong*. The Bridge *the customer is never wrong* is about the courage to challenge your basic assumptions about what is important to the customer. Most often than not, service providers believe that creative advert can help them win the battle for the customer's purse. Maybe, in the short run, but in the long run, the customer is looking for value, service and the need to be treated with respect. When you make a shoddy product and attempt to sell it by guile and creative advert, are you being respectful to the customer? The Customer is Never Wrong.

Though General Motors, Ford and Chrysler were able to narrow the quality gap within 10 years, the damage to the American Automobile industry had become irreversible. According to Edmunds.com, which provides information on the US auto market, Toyota will overtake Ford by mid-2007 in sales volume. Ford thus will slip to become the No. 3 automaker in the United States, while Toyota seizes the No. 2 spot. How has the mighty Ford, which virtually founded the auto industry in 1894, fallen? There is yet more bad news for America auto industry. Fortune magazine of February 27, 2006 in a feature article written by Carol J. Loomis all but concluded that there is the distinct possibility of General Motors going into Chapter 11, short for bankruptcy. And the Fortune magazine of March 13, 2006 concluded its feature article, **How Toyota Does It: The Triumph of The Prius** by Alex Taylor III by saying *"With its huge headstart, better technology, enormous scale, and powerful will to make hybrids an everyday alternative to the internal combustion engine – it's hard to see Toyota not dominating the (auto) industry for years to come"*. In just 45 years (1961 to 2006) Toyota has come from number zero to become the undisputed leader in the auto industry by listening to customers and concluding and truly believing that the customer can never be wrong. And as this book was being rushed to the press, the big three us auto makers were in Washington, cap in hand, begging the US Congress for a $45bn bail out, citing the $60bn bail out to the financial services industry as the justification for their request. Without the bail out, the big three argued, they would all have to go into Chapter Eleven (bankruptcy), thanks to the global economic meltdown! GM did go into Chapter Eleven for 40 days and the Obama administration did dole out the cash and this in no small measure helped the troika of GM, Ford, and Chrysler to restructure and return to profit ways. GM has now emerged from Chapter Eleven, paid off its debts to the US treasury, and together with Ford, are now nimbler and are giving Toyota a good fight for the first time in decades!

Bridge Thirty Nine

KNOW THAT THE CUSTOMER IS MORE IMPORTANT THAN THE CHAIRMAN

Bill Gates was the chairman of Microsoft Corporation until 2004 when he decided to demote himself to Chief Technology Officer. Bill Gates, however, remains one of the richest men in the world. How do Microsoft staff treat or relate to William H. Gates Jr.? Do they tremble whenever he passes by? I doubt.

The customer is more important than the chairman. He is more important than all the board members and general managers. Not long ago the chairman of the corporation was the centre of the universe. Perched atop the organizational pyramid, usually he had a floor to himself, and more often than not, a separate lift. When he passed by, his employees were supposed to genuflect, fake a smile and show respect. It was all part of the power game. No more.

Today, thanks to information technology, everybody is equal. Today, as Francis Bacon foresaw, knowledge is truly power. Today, change is the name of the game and any business that is not able to deliver at the speed of thought will definitely be consigned to the dustbin of history. It all adds up to why the customer is more important than everyone else.

What it takes to survive in today's marketplace is responsiveness. The top management of the business that wants to survive has to strive hard to eliminate all forms of class differences in the work place. No plebeians and aristocrats; no slaves and freeborn. Everybody is equal. Don't look behind your shoulders to see which manager or general manager is around. Focus on the one person that matters: customer.

Diamond Bank is well ahead of the pack on this score, though it still has many miles to travel. In DBL (should be DBP but staff still cling to DBL), as staff call the bank, every body is known by his first name or initial. The bank's founder and founding Chairman go by the initial PGD: for Pascal Gabriel Dozie. To ensure everybody understands that position is nothing, call cards for many years were printed without official designation. For added effect, staff shared offices. Until very recently, it was not uncommon to see two general managers sharing office or an entry level officer sharing office with a senior manager. While the Bank is at the cutting edge of technology, the culture is down to earth. PGD regularly participated in orientation programmes for new staff where he lectured on the origins of the bank, its mission and vision. Everything is laid back until it comes to service.

It is when you take conscious steps to break down all pockets of "bigmanism" in the business that people come to realize that the whole essence of work is service to the customer. And if service is important above all else, then the focus has to be the customer not the 'big man' as you see in most small companies where the founder holds sway.

Bridge Forty

KNOW THAT THE CUSTOMER IS THE KING AND THE BOSS

Yesterday's (call that 19th century) organization chart looked (looks) something like the figure below – twenty stories deep!

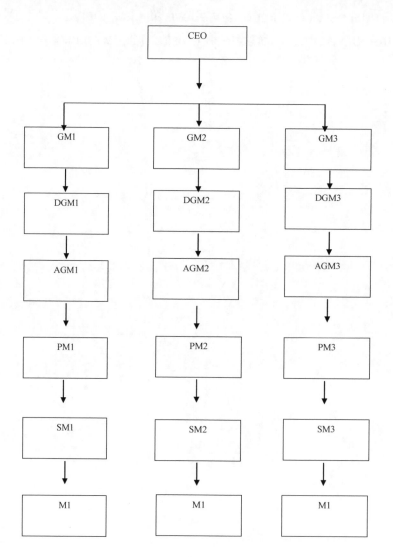

It is called the organigram, organogram, organizational chart and so forth. Here we have stopped at the manager level, in reality, however, it normally goes right down to the gateman! Where is the customer here? With the chart sometimes 20 layers deep, and the CEO sitting in splendid isolation in the penthouse not knowing what is going on - all information is vetted, filtered, altered, tempered with as it meanders through the maze of reporting chain to the top brass - any wonder companies typified by this sort of chart hardly, if ever, offer inspiring service. Many companies are still using this 19th century's organization chart in the 21st century!

Today's organization chart looks something like the chart below:

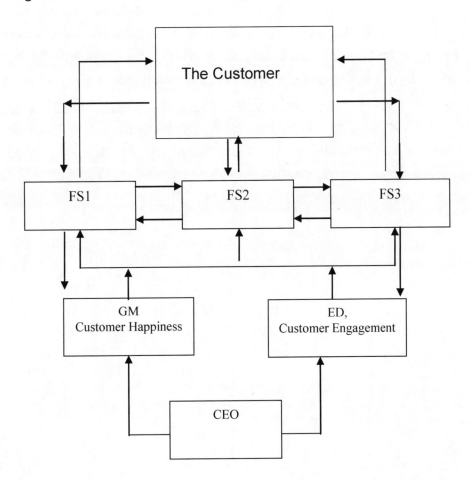

Today's organization chart has the customer as the centre of the universe and the customer facing staff are the most important staff, far more so than the CEO. The job of the CEO is to create an enabling environment for the customer facing staff to go all out and *die* for the customer. Then you must get Director or GM or VP, Customer Happiness and ED or President, Customer Engagement, just as you have ED, Admin, VP Accounts, and GM, Engineering.

According to the authors Robert Spector and Patrick D. McCarthy, Nordstrom uses the 'inverted pyramid' organization chart to reinforce their customer centric leadership style. *"What set Nordstrom apart is that, from department manager to co-chairman, all tiers of the inverted pyramid work to support the sales staff, not the other way round",* the authors stated. Spector and McCarthy further quoted Ray Johnson, retired co-chairman as saying. *"The only thing we have going for us is the way we take care of our customers, and the people who take care of the customers are on the floor."*

Tom Peters in his **Liberation Management** predicts that tomorrow's organization structure will be the " *'amoebae' - ever changing, ever unpredictable, fluid, projectized, the spaghetti organization with total intertwining of people without regard to rank, function or location."* Anarchy! Yes. Will it work? Yes, as sure as CNN, which Peters cites as the quintessential spaghetti organization. Do you ever wonder how CNN manages to cover the entire globe round the clock 24 hours a day, 7 days a week, 365 days a year nonstop since 1980? CNN has been a spaghetti organization from day one with no frontiers, with little or no hierarchy. What makes that possible? The microchip makes that possible. Peters counsels, any time you are tempted to add one more layer to your already extended organization chart, ask, *"will that help the customer's cause?"*

Bridge Forty One

DON'T JUST SATISFY THE CUSTOMER, *COMPLETELY* SATISFY AND *DELIGHT* HER

Tom Peters and Robert Waterman's (Jr.) intoxicating book on quality, **In Search of Excellence,** first published in 1982 brought *Quality* from the closet of the quality control practitioners to the popular domain. The book listed companies that in the reckoning of the authors had reached the zenith of innovativeness and performance and were therefore adjudged excellent. Among them were Bechtel, Boeing, Caterpillar Tractor, Dana, Data General, Delta Airlines, Digital Equipment, Emerson Electric, Fluor, Hewlett-Packard, IBM, Intel, Johnson & Johnson, McDonald's, Procter & Gamble, Texas Instrument, Wang Labs, 3M. Within a few short years after *In Search*, some of the excellent companies had ceased to exist (e.g. Wang), while some had become ghosts of their former selves e.g. IBM. Though some of the companies, like IBM, have clawed their way back after massive reengineering and the replacement of their CEOs (IBM hired Lou Gerstner to take over John Akers job), it all goes to show how slippery the world of excellence can be.

The *Search* began in 1977 or thereabout. Then, of the 62 American companies the authors studied, roughly 36 had what it took to be called excellent. Twenty years on, everybody has *Quality*. The Japanese have it. The Americans have it. The Europeans have it. As Fred Crawley, the then Chairman of Alliance and Leicester Building Society, and Girobank puts it, *'if yesterday quality was a winning ticket, today it's no more than an admission ticket'*. Now the battleground has changed. Satisfying the customer is now no more enough as Deming (1982) and Beskett (1994) have emphasized. Today it is necessary to delight and astound the customer. Tom Peters calls the new paradigm *"The Pursuit of WOW!"*

Amongst global companies, Nordstrom is perhaps the most well known for legendary customer service. **The Nordstrom Way: The Inside Story Of America's #1 Customer**

Service Company by Robert Spector and Patrick D. McCarthy cited variously all over this book is replete with racy stories how Nordstrom's associates (as the staff are called) go out of their way to astound customers. Amongst the numerous stories the one I like most is the one about a certain customer that went to Nordstrom purposely to test the company's vaunted service prowess. The man tempted Nordstrom's claim that suits could be mended within five minutes. And because Nordstrom could not fulfill the order within the stipulated time frame, the man sauntered away fully satisfied that Nordstrom was not that legendary after all. This story would have ended there. However before he left, as William H. Davidow and Bro Uttal graphically recount in their **Total Customer Service: The Ultimate Weapon,** he left behind the details of his hotel, including the room number. Guess what Nordstrom did! Nordstrom FEDEXED the suit to the hotel and it was delivered ahead of his arrival in the hotel. As the man stepped into his hotel room a FEDEX parcel was waiting. He opened it and inside was his suit, two silk ties and a handkerchief, and of course a letter of appreciation. The man was blown away. He believed!

Tom Peters tells a fascinating story about Verifone in his **The Pursuit of WOW!** The story was about how Verifone, which at the time controlled about 60% of the US card authorization market, handled a proposal for a consortium of German banks. Regarded by the author as *"a new model for the economy"* and described as priding itself on a *'culture of urgency'*, Verifone reduced the concept of globalization from a high flaunting jargon to everyday reality in quoting for the contract displaying unmatched responsiveness in the process. This is the story as Peters recounted it. Verifone has offices in Redwood City, Tapei and London, and to ensure the job got done the three offices worked in tandem, such that when staff in Redwood City closed for the day they zapped the job to Tapei, which in turn zapped it to London at the end of their day, and which returned it to Redwood City after their days was over. Peters concluded the amazing story by saying *"Needless to say, Verifone got the order, shocking the bankers and shaming competitors"*. Talk about responsiveness!

Responsiveness is the key to the future. It is no longer news that, thanks to the information superhighway, the world is now a global village, where Anua where I was born is just as close by as Newfoundland, some 20,000 kilometers in another continent, 12 time zones away. With the internet, you could zap a document to a person in another continent just by the click of a mouse, or call the person wherever he may be on the planet using a Thuraya or a common GSM phone with roaming capabilities. Gone are the days when Newfoundland sounded as if it was on another planet. With a super jumbo plane, you could leave Lagos after breakfast and join a business associate in Newfoundland for dinner in the evening of the same day. This world, which continues to shrink as the internet becomes all pervasive, will not tolerate sloppiness.

Every organization must unlearn the old ways of doing business, where replying a letter within two weeks was considered normal; where you could send in your expression of interest or quotation some six weeks after the request. We must all learn the new ways where having an acute sense of urgency is the norm. People everywhere in the organization must learn to work fast; everyone must learn to respond to the customer's every request with lightning speed. This is the only way you can astound the customer. Organizations that continue to operate in the old mode are destined for the museum. NIPOST, NACRBD, Nigerian Railways, Federal Government Ministries, State ministries from Lagos to Maiduguri and from Sokoto to Calabar, Nigerian SMEs must all wake up from their slumber. The world does not owe us a living, rather we owe the world our living. As Tom Peters boldly proclaims in his ***The Circle of Innovation - "YOU CAN'T SHRINK YOUR WAY TO GREATNESS*!"** Replying a letter the same day, attending to government business expressly, repairing failed roads within days, mending broken public water pipe before the business day is over, repairing an unserviceable electricity transformer within hours, we can go on and on are all against the conventional wisdom in Nigeria's public sector. But as an individual employee working in that ministry or agency or parastatal I encourage you to buck that conventional wisdom. Go out there and accomplish the wonders you were created to perform.

Sam Walton in his **Ten Rules That Worked For Me** charged in Rule 10: *"Swim upstream. Go the other way. Ignore the conventional wisdom."* Sam Walton is saying the old methods will not suffice. Do it differently as he did to Wal-Mart when the conventional wisdom was that a 50,000 community wouldn't support the discount store the man was trying to set up. Walton said through out the years he was building his empire, people kept hammering that idea to him. Of course he ignored them and went on to become one of the richest men in the world with Wal-Mart stores all over the world, except in Africa, south of the Sahara.

Bridge Forty Two

EMPOWER YOUR STAFF TO WORK FOR THE CUSTOMER

In **Living the Seven Habits**, Steven Covey captures in graphic detail an episode that would qualify as an instance of the Bridge *empower your staff to work for the customer*. Covey was relating a story as was told by Chris Turner of Xerox Business Services. The story was simple. A bank teller manning a drive-through outlet on a Friday night found herself overwhelmed by requests to encash cheques that she ran out of change. To save the situation she started rounding up to one dollar and then to five dollars and then to ten, ending up with cash shortage of $200 (about N30,000)! She justified her action by saying *"failing to meet customers' needs would have undermined the bank's long-term relationship with the community."* The news media got wind of her action and came up with stories praising her for *"doing the right thing."* What was the bank's reward for this philantrophic effort? The incident ended up being a publicity boon for the bank that it *"signed up a hundred new customers the next week."*

The message is clear. When you focus on what is right for the customers, it pays off in business results. The Bridge *empower your staff to work for the customer* is a subset of the Bridge *focus all decisions on the customer*, but it's much more in that you lose money in the short run. Let your people know that any decision they take, right or wrong, in the genuine belief that they are serving the customers' interest will be supported. When staff are empowered in this positive context, they become even more enterprising in deciding which interest will further the company's cause as a story, which appeared in **NUTS!** by Kevin Freigberg and Jackie Freigberg, from a Southwest airlines elated customer illustrates. The story centered on a Southwest airlines flight Dispatch officer who switched two aircrafts, one billed for Columbus, Ohio, and the other billed for Kansas City, to avert delay of the Columbus bound flight as fog caused a one -hour delay at Cleveland of the inbound aircraft that was due to convey the Columbus bound passengers. The net effect was that despite the one hour delay in Cleveland, the Columbus bound flight still took off on schedule as the aircraft originally billed for Kansas City was used, while the Cleveland aircaft was used for the Kansas City flight. Noting the risk associated with such decisions, only companies with lion hearts give their people the space to take such audacious life and death decisions. The elated customer concluded her letter to Herb Kelleher, Chairman of Southwest airlines with these words *"Flying with Southwest Airlines is a pleasure!"* Wao!

Empower your people to work for the customer and you will be handsomely rewarded. As Tom Peters emphasised in his book, **Tom Peters Seminar**, in Ritz Carlton all room keepers are empowered to spend up to $2,000 to fix customer problems *on the spot* without referring to their supervisors. When you disobey or break the Bridge empower your staff to work for the customer, the opposite happens, you breed turkeys who deliver service by the rule book. You breed emotionally crippled people who refer all customer service problems *up* to the annoyance of the customer and the wasting of everybody's time and energy. The Bridge *empower your staff to work for the customer* is at the heart of this book, without it every other thing becomes that more difficult if not impossible to implement. To gain more power, top management and every body that has the word *manager* attached to his official designation must cede all that power to the people at the frontlines while keeping score. This is the whole essence of empowerment!

Bridge Forty Three

LET THE CUSTOMER BE ABLE TO SAY WOW! ABOUT YOUR SERVICE – BEHIND YOU!

Tom Peters in his **Thriving On Chaos** pointed out that Steve Leonard coined the word 'Wow!'. Stew used the word to express the *"sense of excitement which he (Stew) believed is the essence of the store's achievement."* Now, can you answer 'YES' without any iota of doubt or sense of equivocation, if I were to ask you: is the service your company delivers exhilarating such that your customers can shout WOW! behind your back? Whenever I ask that question at seminars, usually, a cold hush descends on the room because everybody delivers mediocre service. Again, if I were to ask, has a customer written to you within the past 90 days (90 days is too far, don't be kidding), make that 3 days, extolling your people and their service prowess? What would be your answer? Serious, send your answer with the name and address of your company to me through the email address at the end of this book!

Research by Leonard Berry and others have suggested that *"Service quality is relative, not absolute, it is determined by the customer, not by the service provider."* Due to the wide variability of service there are countless permutations to enhancing or augmenting service and what you can really do is only limited by your imagination. Think innovation. Think creativity. Leonard Berry and his colleagues suggest that companies can enhance quality either by meeting and exceeding the expection of customers or by taking steps to lower such expectation. I do not fully agree with the authors' suggestion that controlling customers' expectations can lead to quality for the simple reason that if others are exceeding customers' expectation while you are taking steps to control such expectations customers may just to come to believe that you're out of touch with the times. Which company ever controlled customers' expectations and flourished? Ask GM. Ask Ford. Ask Chrysler. The key really is to *know* the customer. This calls for hard work. It is sometimes futile to try to model a service that will be equally satisfactory to all customers at the same time. You cannot be all things to all men. You have to carefully select your market niche and dominate it in terms of service prowess.

Bridge Forty Four

FIND OUT WHO YOUR CUSTOMER SERVICE HEROES ARE AND WHAT REALLY MAKES THEM TICK

Herb Kelleher! Carl Sewell! Joe Girard! Art Huskey! Stew Leonard! Colin Marshall! Great men all! To them service is everything. Then you have the great companies, such as Nordstrom, Toyota, Ritz Carlton, Wal-Mart, Marriot, FEDEX. Whether you're looking at people or companies, what sets the truly great people and companies apart is their passion for service. But then every company is made up of people. It's people that make companies great. In every great company, you have the truly great service heroes. They are always truly exceptional. Find out what makes them such great people to be with.

We had in another Bridge mentioned the Honda worker who straightens the wiper blade of all Honda cars he sees on his way home from work because he couldn't imagine any thing wrong with a Honda. We also mentioned staff of Frito-Lay that braved mud, sleet, snow, hail and storm to ensure they upheld their team's 99.5% service record to restock customers on time and on schedule. These as we pointed out are stories that Tom Peters told in *In Search of Excellence*. In *The Pursuit of WOW*! Tom said he did what he said had never been done in publishing history: he had pictures of his service heroes published in the book. One of the pictures was that of Virginia Azuela, the housekeeper of the 54th floor of the Ritz Carlton in San Francisco. In the picture, Ms. Azuela was in her duty uniform, holding her carpet cleaning machine and smiling from ear to ear. No doubt every organization has its own Virginia Azuelas who 99.99 per cent of the time go unrecognized but going about all the same delivering outstanding quality service. Your job as a manager is to find out the make up of these service heroes and use what you find as a basis for recruiting and selecting future employees! Recruitment and selection hold the key to outstanding service. The CEO should personally have oversight over the recruitment and selection by having the head of HRM (or HCM if you like) report directly to him.

Bridge Forty Five

NEVER BANG THE PHONE ON THE CUSTOMER

Another trite one! Simplistic you would say. And I agree. The sad fact is it keeps happening every day. Why? Because the typical Nigerian small business will employ any relative of the managing director that comes along, typically the in-law, cousin, sister, brother, you name it. With no training whatsoever, they are literally let loose on the customer.

Consider my experience while trying to find out more details of a seminar for which we were sent a brochure. The brochure carried two phone numbers to call for space reservation. Ordinarily this should have been a straightforward telephone conversation. What I expected at 9 am in the morning was a charming voice, with all the information I needed to make my reservation. I expected a pleasant experience but it turned out to be a journey to nowhere. This is how this transaction proceeded.

Paul: Hi Good Morning, I'm calling from The Best Bank Training School, Apapa; my name is Paul. Is this Lubserve?

Girl: What?

Paul: Is this Lubserve please? And may I know who I'm speaking with?

Girl: What do you want?

Paul: May I know who I'm speaking with?

Girl: Bola! (she mutters incomprehensibles!)

Paul: Bola, please can I make a reservation for the seminar advertised...

Bola: (interrupts) Which seminar?

Paul: Please Bola, what of Engr. …. The brochure I have here….

Bola: (interrupts) Oh! Engr. ……,he is not around.

Paul: Bola, kindly tell Engr. … about this call. He can reach me on 01-580-5405.

Engr. Big Shot did call five hours later, so you can say I was lucky. My staff, Eric, was not that lucky. He had called the Industrial Training Fund, Ikeja, to inquire about their head office address in Jos. On the other end was a lady who said she did not know the head office address and there was nothing she could do. If my staff called back anytime, he could get the address from any other person. The final dialogue went thus:

Eric:	Please, when can I call back?
Unknown ITF staff:	Anytime.
Eric:	Please who do I ask for?
Unknown ITF staff:	Just ask for anybody around, they will give you the number.
Eric:	But what is your name?
Unknown ITF staff:	I've already told you I don't know the number. I won't give you my name.

Of course, it was a losing proposition. My staff had to give up. You can say he was equally lucky, for the girl did not bang the phone on him. Only a complete idiot would bang the phone on a customer. But this is a common occurrence. Sometimes you have supposedly professional people indirectly banging the phone on you because you are wasting their time. What you have to know is that not everybody is very articulate and coherent on phone. Your work as a phone operator, call centre staff or whatever the nomenclature is to lead the caller to ensure the objective of the call is achieved by asking questions, probing and gently leading the caller to arrive at a decision. Management needs to put the most articulate and friendly people at the call centre.

Dell Computers in 2006 reorganized its call centre and instituted new metrics for measuring the effectiveness of its call centre staff. Before then call centre staff were rated on how quickly they completed calls, the faster the better no matter whether a problem was resolved or not as cost was the primary consideration. The tendency was for call centre staff to literally stop callers on their track as they strived to limit the duration of calls. In short they banged phones on customers. Complaints soared. Michael Dell accepted blame when he told Fortune they realized they were wrong in using call duration for measuring the productivity of call centre staff. Going forward call centre staff would be appraised on how effectively customers' problems are resolved. It takes tremendous courage to acknowledge such mistakes and take corrective action.

Bridge Forty Six

DON'T DO IN ROME AS THE ROMANS DO IN CUSTOMER SERVICE – EXCEED THE ROMANS

You just cannot succeed in today's business world by doing what everybody else is doing, you have to be completely different. Recall in the 2009 edition of Bridges, I talked about my one-time neighbor who in 1999 opened a restaurant and I was invited to attend the "launching". I also mentioned that within a mile radius of my neighbor's restaurant were not less than twenty other restaurants, fast foods and nightly eateries including Mr. BIGGS, Tantalizers, Kas Chicken (now dead), Pintos (now dead), Sweet Sensation and Tastee Fried Chicken. My neighbor believed her culinary prowess would enable her succeed and thrive but I said at the time I doubted she would survive. I said in that edition that the odds of her succeeding were one in ten or slimmer because what she was offering was not different from all the other eatries around her were offering. Well, what I feared indeed came to pass and the restaurant went belly-up and my neighbor did the next logical thing: she packed her bag and baggages and left for the US.

Bridge Forty Six *Don't Do In Rome As The Romans Do In Customer Service – Exceed The Romans* is about standing out from the crowd. What makes you distinctive? What have you done and continue to do day in and day out so that anytime the people that you consider as your target market want to do anything tangentially associated with the business which you have entered, they think about you first and no one else. This is called *positioning* as Al Ries & Jack Trout brilliantly captured in their best seller **Positioning** and further illustrated its application in **The 22 Immutable Laws of Marketing.** Have you positioned yourself so that you are the first in the customers mind at all times? Think about it. Why should I go to KAS Chicken and not MR. BIGGS? Because KAS Chicken (now dead though) stayed open till 12 midnight while MR. BIGGS closed at 8.30 pm and in some places, at 7pm. That's why! KAS Chicken died because the founder got her attention diverted to other things but staying open as late as 12 midnight in a city that supposedly should never sleep while MR BIGGS operated its outlets as an extension of Lagos State Ministry of Environment and Physical Planning was a brilliant idea.

Carl Sewell, author (with Paul brown) of **Customers for Life** took his father's moribund car dealership to stratospheric success by refusing to do in Rome as the Romans do. Tom Peters and Nancy Austin graphically captured in **Passion for Excellence** what Carl Sewell did to turn Sewell Village Cadillac from an *also ran* to best-in- class. *"When he took over the business, he asked, 'Who are the best car dealers in the country?'. He got their names and off he went. He visited, and visited some more. He listened, took notes."* Carl Sewell didn't stop at visiting car dealerships. He visted restaurants, airlines, pizza stores, hotels, and just about any place he could get superior ideas to turn around his dealership. The research aspects concluded, Carl Sewell went back and adapted what he learnt from pizza stores, airlines, restaurants, other car delerships, until one day he became best in class. Carl Sewell never said what works in pizza stores cannot work in a car dealership. He did not say but car dealership is different from airlines. He did not say, this is the way things have always been done in the car dealership industry. He exceeded the Romans and this helped Sewell Village Cadillac to stand out a clear leader in an industry that is known for mediocrity and generally lacking in credibility.

Bridge Forty Seven

LET THE CUSTOMER SEE 1,000 CENTERS OF *EXCELLENCE* IF YOU ARE A 1,000-MAN COMPANY

Quality is not a department! Quality is you and I. Quality is the Chairman, CEO, General Manager, senior, middle and junior managers. Quality is everybody. Quality is the spirit that animates everything that everybody does in the company. Quality is a mindset that says hey, we're here for the customer and we're going to do all that it takes to ensure we deliver. Quality is everybody's business.

In organizations large and small the quality 'revolution' is catching on. But what do you see? In all but the really *excellent* companies, quality is centralized in the *quality department*, so it becomes that Department's child, and besides that, the senior people do not live by the quality tenets. This atmosphere breeds cynicism. People begin to give *eye service.* Quality becomes internally focused. People begin to do the minimum to satisfy what the *quality manual* says. Quality becomes a mechanical book affair. Here quality is lacking in meaning. Everybody may have batches with big *Q* inscribed on them; the company may even fill forms for the Deming or Malcolm Baldridge Award or may have even won one, but *Quality* will still sound hollow when it's not embedded in the culture.

Bridge Forty Eight

ANTICIPATE THE CUSTOMER'S NEXT NEED AND PROVIDE IT BEFORE HE ASKS

The story, perhaps apocryphal, is told of one of Nigeria's early ministers in the first republic who was *forced* to drink 30 cups of tea (some say 50) while attending his very first international summit. The hotel attendant simply refilled the honorable minister's tea cup each time he finished his tea. The process continued until it's said an aid noticed what has going on and went to the victim's aid. He is said to have whispered to the honorable minister to put his cup upside down after downing the last serving. The table attendant was simply following, robot-like, Bridge Forty Eight: *Anticipate The Customer's Next Need And Provide It Before He Asks*. It is claimed that table attendants in the world-class hotels always refill the cup immediately it's empty. In that case, it's argued, you don't down your water or tea, you sip. Well!

Bridge Forty Nine

KNOW YOUR COY'S VISION STATEMENT BUT GIVE THE CUSTOMER YOUR PERSONAL ACTION STATEMENT

Our vision is bla bla bla bla bla bla, it rambled on and on and ended with the fact that it wished to be the best telecoms company in the world. That was former NITEL's vision statement, one full page long, it hung in every NITEL's office gathering dust. NITEL was a bad dream. The moribund Nigeria Telecommunications company has now been sold to Transcorp. Many organizations are like NITEL. They have grandiose vision statement, which the management doesn't even believe in, let alone the staff.

Vision statement, yes, now every organization has it. It is supposed to set a concentrated agenda for the organization, pointing to the general direction the organization should be heading. It is a compass of sorts. Michael Kami once said *''a company without a vision is like a ship without a rudder, moving round in circles, it's a tramp, it has no where to go.''* The holy writ even says *'without a vision the people perish.'* Stephen Covey greatly distilled the essence of vision in both the corporate and individual settings in his **Seven Habits of Highly Effective People**. Covey says that vision does the following: *"a) clarifies purpose, b) gives direction, c) empowers us to perform beyond our resources, d) bonds people together, e) becomes the constitution, the criterion for decision making, and f) provides great strength at times of uncertainty."*

But your vision is no more than hot air if you don't translate it into great action. Vision should be entirely action oriented as opposed to being a great statement to be hung on a wall. Vision should stir emotions, and engender great attitude in people. Martin Luther King Jr.'s vision was dignity of the black man, equality, humane society. Though he eschewed, violence he preached action all the way, for instance when he enthused *"If a man is called to be a street sweeper, he should sweep the street even as Michelangelo painted, Beethoven composed music, Shakespeare wrote poetry.*

He should sweep the street so well that all the hosts of heaven and earth will pause to say, here lived a great street sweeper who did his job well." As Carl Mays, the motivational speaker puts it, *"when you're able to do a common thing uncommonly, the word gets out."*

Tom Peters' **Thriving On Chaos**, appropriately sub-titled **Handbook for a Management Revolution,** harped 100 per cent on action. So get on with action not lofty, grandiose words. Without a bias for action your vision statement will end up a big joke, to say the least. In the numerous examples of action orientation of the grocer Stew Leonard's, Peters provides graphic examples how Stew Leonard translated words into action. Leonard, Peters pointed out in one instance, used to have his philosophy displayed on the store's wall. The two philosophies are: *"RULE 1: THE CUSTOMER IS ALWAYS RIGHT. RULE 2: IF THE CUSTOMER IS EVER WRONG, REREAD RULE 1".* Stew Leonard was not entirely satisfied it would seem so he went a step further to concretise his action. He had the two rules written on heavy granite and planted on the store's entrance as a constant reminder to himself and the entire organization. As Stew put it, according to Peters: *'Every time a customer walks by it, they are reminded that that's how they should judge us. We'd better live up to it. There is no place to hide.'* That is what I call action. Any wonder Stew Leonard's ended up in the Guinness Book of World Records, as we earlier mentioned, as the store with the largest sales per square foot for a single grocery store.

Bridge Fifty

KNOW THAT IN CUSTOMER SERVICE NOTHING IS IMPOSSIBLE

He ran 145 miles in 2 days to seek reinforcement. His personal survival was at stake. Not only that, the survival of the entire Athenian city-state and the race was at stake. He had to succeed. Failure was a fate too gruesome to contemplate. The 300 gallant Athenians had held the two-foot wide pass against the 5,000-man strong Persian forces for 45 days, now they had reached the limits of their endurance. Without reinforcement, the defense would collapse. Only the lone marathoner could save the country. His name was Pheidippides, supposedly a messenger, he ran from the plains of Marathon to Sparta to seek Spartan help. It is said that he fell down and died immediately he accomplished his mission. The year was c480 BC. There are many spins to this story! Some have it that Pheidippides ran back to announce Athens's victory, but the key lesson really is the great sense of duty and history Pheidippides displayed. The lesson is simple: in customer service, nothing is impossible. Bridge Fifty is more a state of mind than anything else. This state of mind has to be planted and cultivated as part of the corporate culture.

The following story from the second issue, 1999, of Diamond Bank News captures succinctly that nothing is impossible in customer service philosophy. The story was recounted by Chinelo Nduba, then a staff of Diamond Bank. Diamond Bank was one of the pioneers of the early charge cards, then called Diamond *Paycard* (now rested). Chinelo was in the office on a Saturday morning when a thoroughly agitated and near hysterical customer walked in. His problem: he couldn't use his *Paycard*. The customer had loaded all the money he had on the card, but unknown to him on the day he wanted to use the card it had expired. As noted, it was a weekend, the customer had no cash, he was expecting visitors that weekend, and the branch didn't offer weekend banking, the card had expired. Chinelo was his only hope. Chinelo began by saying "*I told him that there was very little I could do since the branch did not offer*

Saturday banking service." Along the line Chinelo had her *Damascus experience*! She decided to read the balance in the Paycard and discovered that it had a balance of N50,000. On enquiry the customer said he needed just N25,000. To save the day, and with the understanding that the man would replenish the full amount spent, Chinelo gave the customer her own *Paycard*, which incidentally also had a balance of N50,000 thus enabling the man to do his shopping. The customer, it turned out was an IT top brass. He left Chinelo his home and office addresses and cell phone number. The Monday following, the customer was early in the office and returned the card fully replenished. He left Chinelo with a thank you note. Chinelo concluded her story thus *"I couldn't help thinking what a great people Nigerians are! In retrospect, I feel swell to have been of assistance to him, especially in the line of duty."* Well said! From the initial *"there was very little I could do"*, Chinelo recovered spectacularly to save the day for the customer that was obviously stranded! It bears repeating, in customer service, nothing is impossible!

PART 3

CULTIVATING CUSTOMER LOYALTY & RETENTION

Bridge Fifty One

FIND OUT HOW MANY CUSTOMERS YOU ARE LOSING

As the CEO do you know how many customers your company has? Does everybody in the company know on the minute by minute basis how many customers the company has? Do you know how much each of those customers is contributing to your bottom line profit?

Except the very best companies, most organizations do not know the number of customers they have, much less of the contribution of each of those customers make to their profit. What they do is that they look at the total sales and total profit figures at the end of the quarter, and if it is high, they beat their chest and congratulate the senior management and if it is low, they look for a scapegoat to blame, usually some hapless officer down the line.

The other side of the coin of the number of customers you have is the number of customers you're losing. If you do not know the number of customers that you have, chances are that you will not know the number of customers you're losing. At an in-house seminar at one bank (name withheld) in 1998, one of the marketing officers in describing her customer base said she had about 300 customers, but out of that number, only about 30 were really active. She said she did not know most of her customers by name but she believed most of the accounts were dormant. Out of the entire portfolio, only ten percent was really active! Ninety percent could not be accounted for. Ninety per cent of customers had probably switched banks and the account officer did not even know! You just need to multiply those figures by the number of marketing officers in the bank to know the level of leakage. The leakage rate can be staggering! The bank might say it has 10,000 customers, when in reality, it has less than ten percent of those! The truth is, the customer is always judging you: how you treat her, how you take decisions on issues concerning her, whether you care or not, and so forth. If the customer decides that you don't really care, she will leave. As Thomas O. Jones and W. Earl Sasser Jr. highlighted in their seminal HBR paper, **Why Satisfied Customers Defect**, customer may leave you *"in harder-to-spot dribs and drabs or spurts."* The authors cited the case of a bank that may lose a major customer after an account officer that the customer had a good relationship leaves.

Sometimes, the customer will not leave, but she will not be committed to you. If she has no better alternative, she may decide to spread her 'risk' or reduce her level of sacrifice by having accounts in three or five other banks. She of course may leave you outright if she can get better service elsewhere. If not, she may remain and only bring you marginal patronage when she knows her level of sacrifice will be minimal. The important thing to know is that the number of permutations the customer has is limitless. The customer knows since she can always vote with her feet, the crown will always be on her head. The customer is king is not just a cliché, it's a fact of life.

It is important that you continually research to know the number of customers you are losing, the reason for their leaving and what you can do to bring them back. A survey by Mckinsey and Company titled *"Why Industrial Companies Lose Customers"* found that among the reasons customers stopped doing business with their former companies, company indifference (68%), was cited as the most important reason for leaving, while other factors such as lower price else where, and relocation, to mention a few, ranked far below at 9 per cent and 3 per cent, respectively. Knowing why your customer left you makes sense because it enables you to know how you measure up compared to the company he has left to. It enables you ask hard and uncomfortable questions about the level of service you are providing.

Frederick F. Reichheld in his **The Loyalty Effect**, estimates that *"on average, U.S. corporations now lose half their customers in five years, half their employees in four, and half their investors in less than one."* This huge rate of customer defection is not peculiar to the U.S. alone, it is a worldwide phenomenon, as everywhere, we experience industrial and service over capacity and the general transformation of sellers' market to buyers' market. The customer that has left you is not likely to recommend his associates to your company; he is not going to recommend his family members so cultivating customer loyalty makes both financial and economic sense.

Bridge Fifty Two

KNOW THE COST OF LOSING A CUSTOMER

Knowing how many customers you're losing (bridge fifty one) is the first leg of this equation. Ask yourself, how did I get these customers in the first place? You will realize that you probably *marketed* actively via advertisement, promotions, sponsorship and in other innumerable ways. So losing a single customer means you're losing money. In its research, the **Technical Assistance Research Programme** (TARP) Institute in the US reported that *"each customer retained by a bank for five years equated to roughly $263 in profits."* TARP further estimated that it costs five times more to get a new customer than to retain an existing one. It therefore makes sense to retain existing customers, who already know you, than running after new ones. A summary of TARP findings indicated that about 95% of people that have bad service experience don't complain, they simply walk away. Of this number, 13% tell up to 20 people about their bad service experience. The same TARP research indicated that a satisfied customer on the average tells only five people.

Don't forget the TARP research was before the internet era. Today where news can circle the world a million times at the speed of light via Facebook, YouTUBE, Twitter, and all sorts of internet newsgroups, you dare to mess up with the customer at your own peril as United Airlines found out when it messed up Dave Carroll's acoustic Taylor guitar in 2008 and refused to apologise and pay compensation. Carroll did what he knows how to do best. He wrote a song about his experience with United Airlines and released the video on YouTube. Within 10 days nearly 4 million had watched the video and United's shares fell 10%, losing a massive $180mm in value. The title of the song: United Breaks Guitars. It quickly climbed to number 20 on Canada's iTunes top hits. Listen to the song and view the video at www.DaveCarroll.com/song3. United is now suing for peace which the Canadian born singer has rebuffed. Be warned!

Laurie Liswood, a one time assessor for the Malcolm Baldridge National Quality Award in her book **Serving Them Right**, gave the *'total cost'* of losing and replacing

150 customers to be $60,000. She puts the *'full financial bottom line impact'* of a bank losing 1,000 accounts at $235,000. These are extremely conservative figures, Laurie asserts, for it does not take into account the loss in morale your staff will experience. It does not take into account the negative publicity you will get. Above all, it does not take into account the negative communication from the lost customers.

Bridge Fifty Two puts before you the stark reality of the cost of poor quality. In essence, cost of quality, or put it in another way, the cost of poor quality is the price you pay for continuing to run your business the old fashion way. You only need to add the cost of quality from the different units of your company to realize that you're bleeding slowly to death by not enthroning quality as your number one objective. Most organizations do not know the full significance of the cost of losing a customer and in their ignorance accept these costs as part of the 'cost of doing business' in the first place. But it's not.

Phillip Crosby, in his book **Quality is Free**, estimates that manufacturing companies spend up to 20 per cent of their profit *'doing things wrong and doing them all over again.'* For service companies, he estimates that the cost of quality can be as high as 40 per cent of sales revenue. With this awareness in mind, get to work. Find out how many customers you're losing. Find out how many customers are not committed to you. Find out those that are indifferent to you. Find out the cost to you of losing these customers. If it costs you so much, does it make sense not to be concerned?

Bridge Fifty Three

REWARD CUSTOMER LOYALTY

Do you as CEO know how many customers your company has? Does every staff know on a consistent basis how many customers the company has, the mix of those customers, how many years each has been doing business with you, the volume of that business and the profitability of each and everyone of those customers? Most often than not, organizations do not have such information on a consistent basis. The information is there quite alright, but is scattered in the various units of the company or reside in various individuals. And because of the in-built barriers to communication in the typical company, the information is not readily available to those that need it, when they need it. Any wonder then that you don't know your valuable customers let alone know how valuable they are?

Banks are notorious for not rewarding customer loyalty. Some banks will close your account if it remains "inactive" for any considerable length of time, and they won't warn you about it. Banks have their reason for closing inactive accounts, but the customer should be forewarned and serious effort made to find out why the account went into dormancy. Laura Liswood captures the absolute necessity for rewarding customer succinctly in her **Serving Them Right.** Using the example of a bank, Liswood reasons that if a customer has been faithful to you over the years without any problem it makes no sense to bounce that customer's cheque for a minor infrngement without making attempt to find out what may have happened. The customer may have travelled, or something may have happened that altered the customer's usual routine. The bank may be quick to blame their systems but what you are telling the customer really Liswood says is "*we are interested in you* *when all is well, we do not appreciate your loyalty, in fact, we do not even know about it.*" This obviously is not the right way to reward customer loyalty. Banks as I earlier said are the worst 'fair weather' friends and I believe this is what led George Bernard Shaw to say "*a banker is someone who gives you his umbrella when the sun is shining and wants it back the moment it begins to rain.*"

Bridge Fifty Four

MAKE CUSTOMER RETENTION AN IMPORTANT THEME IN YOUR MANAGEMENT MEETINGS

Where your treasure lies, there your mind is. It sounds incredibly simple. Put the customer first. Find out how they feel about your business. Just take care of the customer, and the business will take care of itself. Hey, this is old stuff, we all know this. True nothing new here. In fact, there is nothing new under the sun. But, how often in your company do you sit down to discuss the customer?

Ninety percent of organizations don't even know how many customers they have let alone discuss the customer. They will discuss everything else except the customer. Top on the agenda of the things they discuss is the quarterly profit, balance sheet size, return on assets, and return on equity, deposit per staff, you name it. Once in a year, they have end of year retreat where they review the performance for the previous year and map out new strategies how they can increase their market share. But as you and I know, profit, market share and other financial indicators are all lagging indicators - they only tell you what you have done in the past. They are ends by themselves. They tell you nothing about tomorrow. Only the customer can do that.

How you got to where you are, how much profit you make and whether your market share is contracting or expanding depend on the customer. The customer is the means to those profits. It makes sense to discuss the customer. How many have we gained lately? How many have we lost? Are we the organization of first choice? If not, why not? Do customers feel they are being appreciated? How many have complained recently? What did they complain about? What did we do about it? Were they satisfied? Of the lot, how many were delighted? Do we in the executive know the top 10, 50, 100, 1,000 customers? What have we done for them lately? Are we making life simple for them?

These sorts of questions give you insight as to why your market share is growing or shrinking. The customer is the cause of your market share growth or decline. The exact percentage of market share you achieve is the effect of your customer retention strategies. You must distinguish the cause from the effect. It is the duty of senior management to pose and answer these critical questions and find answers to them. The best forum to ask them is at the regular management meeting. Just as you discuss strategy, staff matters, major acquisitions, discuss also the customer. Peter Drucker has said, everything you do in the business must be done from the 'outside-in', that is, from the point of view of the customer. Every management meeting should start and end with discussion of the customer.

Bridge Fifty Five

NEVER LOSE AN EXISTING CUSTOMER - IT COSTS MUCH MORE TO ACQUIRE A NEW ONE

A study by Satrix Consulting Group, based in Amsterdam, as quoted by The Economist, found that the life expectancy of the average European and Japanese company is less than 13 years. On the other hand, the study found that Stora, a Swedish paper and chemicals giant, dates back to the 13th century. Other 'living companies' include Japan's Sumitomo (now over 400 years old), America's Du Pont (over 200) and Britain's Pilkington (over 175).

According to the author of **The Loyalty Effect**, Frederick F. Reichheld, *"companies now lose, and have to replace, 50 per cent of their customers in five years, 50 per cent of their employees in four and 50 per cent of their investors in less than one."* It is three to six times cheaper to retain existing customers than to attract new ones according to Thomas O. Jones, co-founder of Epsilon. The Technical Assistance Research Programme (TARP) Institute in the US reported that each customer retained by a bank for over five years equated to roughly $263 in profits. Laura Liswood, a one time examiner for the Malcolm Baldridge Award says losing a customer usually has a *"domino effect"*. She has calculated the average cost of acquiring 1,000 customers by a bank to be $235,000. According to her, it costs $60,000 to loss and replace 150 customers. With this grim statistics, do you still need someone to tell you to hold on tightly to your existing customers?

Bridge Fifty Six

BUILD ENDURING RELATIONSHIP WITH THE CUSTOMER

We earlier quoted George Bernard Shaw as saying *"a banker is someone who gives you his umbrella when the sun is shining and wants it back the moment it begins to rain."* Your customer is 19, female. She started work a month ago and plans to get married in the next three years. Assume you're a banker and she decides to open an account with your bank, how would you manage the relationship? The idea you should ponder is: will this young lady's children grow up to bank with our bank? Fine, you will not be there 23 years down the road. But it's something to ponder about.

How do you build relationships? Do you go for the quick kill or do you nurture it? The Bridge *Build Enduring Relationship with the Customer* is about loyalty. Management expert Frederick F. Reichheld has written extensively on loyalty. His book **The Loyalty Effect** was devoted to the whole idea of keeping customer for live. Toyota the Japanese car manufacturing giant has the long term vision of keeping for live any person that ever buys a Toyota and is working tirelessly to realize the vision.

The idea of building enduring relationship is not new at all. Marketers call it "relationship marketing". It requires taking inside-out customer-focus approach to every single thing you do. How can we do it better? What did we do last time that can be improved upon? As the customer grows through the natural life cycle, what do we need to do to guarantee we remain relevant to her ever changing needs? These are the sort of questions you need to ask to continuously focus your mind on the next twist and turn in this relationship that should never end.

Building enduring relationship with the customer, whether you are talking about the internal or the external customer is no rocket science. Organizations make costly mistake when they lay off their staff in the most cavalier manner when managing such transitions should be occasions to display grace, dignity and empathy. Some companies go to the extent of calling the staff being laid off dead woods! The staff being laid off were once colleagues for God's sake so why rub salt on injury. Needless to say such lay offs require delicate handling, with the company arranging soft loans for such staff if at all possible, paying their severance entitlement immediately, arranging befitting send off, keeping in touch with the ex-staff and inviting them to company events for as long as they live, automatically admitting all ex-staff to their ex-staff alumni association. And much more. The permutations are limitless.

For customers the array of things you can do is also limitless. For a starter, think of a magazine devoted strictly to customers. Invite customer to submit articles. Think of customers' picnics, paid for by customers. The company just provides the *social umbrella* for the customers to network and socialise. Think of inviting customers and their near relatives to visit key functional areas of your company to see how staff work. Or think of just bringing them home once a year for hot dogs and beer. Why not? I read with elation how General Motor's Saturn Division handled such a 'homecoming' festival for Saturn owners. In 1994 all Saturn owners across the US and Canada were invited to Spring Hill, Teneessee, where the car is made and an estimated 30,000 of them turned up. According to Tom Peters, the reception included *"country music, factory tours, dancing, eating and drinking."* Later Saturn research, claimed Peters, showed that *"60 per cent of current Saturn owners intend to buy another Saturn."* It is this cult-like devotion to a brand or a company that we are talking about in the Bridge *Build Enduring Relationship with the Customer*

Building enduring relationship is particularly important in banking. For emphasis sake, we will repeat Laura A Liswood's words for she captured this eloquently in her **Serving Them Right** when she said when we don't value the customer's loyalty, *"the message you have sent to the customer is we are interested in you when all is well, we do not really appreciate your loyalty, in fact, we do not even know about it."* George Bernard Shaw was right when he joked that a *'banker is someone who gives you his umbrella when the sun is shining and wants it back the moment it begins to rain.'*

Top management and staff always have to be alert to the customer-satisfaction implications of all the company's SOPs (standard operating procedures) and policies. There are a number of simple but effective actions that will show customers the bank really cares about what happens to them. Nigerian banks are now quite adept at this as the average bank now sends out birthday cards, christmas gifts, and generally participate in their customer's special annivessaries. They send text messages, emails or automatic alerts to their customers to confirm the accuracy or authenticity of transactions. Yet at the business or corporate level, a bank can send staff from their advisory unit to a customer when they observe the customer's account performance has started dwindling. The customer may have fallen into hard times or my have simply diverted its business elsewhere without the bank knowing. The simple process of keeping a close eye on the customer's account performance and taking immediate action whenever the account performance falls below expectation can save numerous account relationships.

Though many so-called new generation banks now send birthday cards, and sometimes presents to their important customers and members of their families, the old generation banks are yet to awake to this new wind that is blowing. Using information technology each customer's birthday appears on the computer screen once the account is accessed. Citibank, before it became Citigroup, regularly checked its customers' accounts continuously on measures of ART, namely, *Accuracy, Responsiveness* and *Timeliness.* Joe Girard, the greatest car salesman according to the Guinness Book of World Records has estimated that offending one customer could translate to offending 70,000 people, a whole stadium-full, through the application of the law of 250! Carl Sewell, the Cadillac Czar, we earlier mentioned has estimated that the lifetime value of a customer buying automobile to be $336,000 (about N48.72mm at the current exchange rate) so building enduring relationship with the customer makes perfect economic sense. You cannot, of course, achieve any meaningful payback when you approach customer service as an add-on, supported with flavour of the month actions as birthday cards. What we are talking about are initiatives that address the very foundations of the relationship from the date the relationship begins, tracking the customer's life cycle, transiting to his/her children and children children. This is the concept of the *family bank* built on a solid foundation of mutual trust and transperancy.

Bridge Fifty Seven

KNOW THAT NO CUSTOMER IS DISPENSABLE

Are customers always right? *''No they are not''*, Kelleher snaps. Kelleher went on to say that carrying wrong passengers, and from the context of the discussion, those that abuse staff is *"the biggest betrayals of your people"*. In Kelleher's words *" 'The customer is frequently wrong. We don't carry those sorts of customers. We write them and say, 'Fly somebody else. Don't abuse our people.'"* Tom Peters, writing in his **The Pursuit of WOW**!, recalling an interview with Herb Kelleher, the legendary founding chairman of Southwest Airlines.

Southwest Airlines redefined how air traveling should be – no frills. I love Herb Kelleher for his no-nonsense management style and for all else that he stood for. Herb passionately loved his people, and the people of Southwest Airlines truly loved him. I am an Herb fanatic. I love his no-frills approach to air travel. In this one instance, however, I disagree with Herb. No customer is ever wrong. And as Tom would say, *"PERIOD!"* The customer may be mistaken in his perception or ideas. The customer may be frustrated, but our singular duty is to actively engage her and change that mistaken perception and end up having a happy and delighted customer. It bears to repeat that the customer who leaves his home and comes to your business premises to do business with you certainly wishes you well. Don't antagonize that customer.

I believe that if you look very well at all the problems your company is facing you will discover that 100 per cent of the time, they are self-inflicted. Take the case of an airline. Your advertisement may say your departure is 100 per cent on schedule, all your aircraft are equipped with state-of-the-art in-flight entertainment and your cuisine is the best the world has to offer. And the customer reaches his destination and discovers that his baggage has been sent elsewhere or is missing altogether. Should the customer go home and be happy because you gave him such terrific in-flight film and three course meal?

Allow the customer to complain. It's good for you to know what you can improve immediately. If you train your people well, they will be able to handle the situation professionally. Sometimes all that is required is to say 'sorry'. No customer is dispensable. How would it feel to open your doors for business and for one full day no customer showed up and you received no telephone call? Do you feel happy because your office floors have marble tiles and all your staff have the latest iMac computers? Don't kid yourself. The equation is simple: No customer = No Sales = No Business. It's that simple. That is why Toyota's philosophy as we earlier pointed out is '' Customer first, dealer second, company third.'' That is why Toyota will ever remain one of the greatest companies on earth or the entire universe! Despite its vehicle recall woes in the US (over 8.4mm recalled at the last count), in a recent poll, customers affirmed they will buy Toyota when its time to buy a new car. Such is the power of the Toyota brand. Do you put your executive directors first and customers second in your company? Think!

PART 4

MEASURE! MEASURE!! MEASURE!!!

Bridge Fifty Eight

SET STANDARD FOR EVERY CUSTOMER SERVICE CONTACT POINT AND MONITOR HOW YOU'RE PERFORMING

Customer service contact points, what are those? Before I proceed, let me share my recent experience with Institute of Financial Services (*IFS*), formerly, The Chartered Institute of Bankers (CIB), London. I had to apply for reinstatement to membership, my name having been removed from the register of members for owing one year's subscription. This necessitated sending reinstatement fees to the IFS. The fees were sent in June and for more than one month there was no acknowledgement. A phone call confirmed the fees had been received. After two months I sent a fax for a formal confirmation but there was no acknowledgement. In the middle of November I received a magazine from IFS and a letter confirming my reinstatement. There was no apology for delay. The letter was dated 28 September, 1998 and signed Customer Services. Before I lost my membership I'd been a member of IFS for twelve years.

My letter was the contact point with the IFS. You may already know what customer service contact point is but should you bother about how you perform at those points? The simple answer is, yes. To the customer, those contact points constitute your company. To the customer, the company *is* whoever at wherever the customer has to transact business with. And in today's world the time is 24/7/365. When the customer has an unpleasant experience, he says first and foremost, look at what XYZ company did to me and not what staff Paul of XYZ company did to me.

The customer's overall impression about your company is formed at the service contact points while interacting with your company. The points at which the customer makes contact with your company have come to be aptly described as '*the moments of truth*', first coined by Jan Carlzon, the then CEO of SAS (Scandinavian Airline Systems), in his racy book of the same title. And moments of truth they truly are.

Your telephone response time, letter turnaround time, the time it takes your staff to make eye contact with the customer, complaints handling responsiveness, the list is endless, say more about your company than anything else. The taste of the pudding they say is in the eating. Your elegant advertisement which says you care for the customer 100% and you are the best company under the sun amounts to nothing if it takes staff ages to answer the phone. In our nanoseconds world, three telephone rings is like eternity. You must answer the phone at just one ring.

It is imperative that unambiguous standards are set for each and every customer-service-contact-point and sanctions for breaches spelt out in black and white. The standards and accompanying sanctions should be consistently monitored with a view to implementing continuous and never ending improvement. Some organizations have these standards. Some publish them in colour using the best glossy papers available. Some call theirs *Customer Service Charter* while others call theirs *Customer Service Manual*. Some call theirs the *Service Creed*. And what do the companies do with them? They give them to their managers who promptly lock them up in their drawers.

Customer Contact Service Standards should not be locked up in managers' drawers but in the hearts and minds of each and every individual executive and staff. Adherence to the standards, while every ones job, should be the responsibility of designated customer service champions who have been trained on what and how to monitor. In addition to in-house monitoring, independent monitors, such as *mystery shoppers* should be employed to supply additional feedback to management. This can be topped up with market research, all geared towards compiling strategic information and indices for implementing a never-ending improvement – what the Japanese call *kaizen*. Tom Peters espouses revolution and obliteration of the old order but it turns out *kaizen* - orderly, planned and strategically implemented continuous improvement is more in tune with human nature than a revolution as Toyota has consistently demonstrated.

Bridge Fifty Nine

CONDUCT REGULAR ON-GOING CUSTOMER SERVICE SURVEYS

Customer service surveys give you feedback on where you stand in the eyes of the customer. Surveys give you information on how much ground you have covered. The information from surveys enable you measure your relative improvement on the quality journey over time. Unless you measure, you cannot determine the gaps to be bridged. Without measurement, you are like a ship without a rudder - moving round in circles.

More often than not, organizations delude themselves into believing that their service is fantastic because the popular press says so. Sometimes, companies are given awards for *Excellence* by some mushroom institutions of no consequence giving them a false sense of achievement. The awards come in different forms - plagues, laminated certificates, medals and cups. Companies make a great show of this achievement, organizing press conferences and expensive dinner to blow their trumpets, while their service remains at best mediocre. This is self delusion. Unless your customers say so, you cannot claim your service is fantastic. Motorola is a great company. It was one of the first companies to win the coveted Malcolm Baldridge National Quality Award, and is today one of the key exponents of six-sigma, however, all these have not helped Motorola much as it continues to lose market share to Nokia and was recently relegated to number three position globally by Samsung. What we are saying in effect is that only the customer, that is, the market place is the only true arbiter in the quest for share of minds and wallet, and not awards per se. In the market place, majority of customers genuinely believe Nokia phones are more durable and customer friendly. The first GSM phone I had was Motorola V50. The screen turned black nearly every three months. In the one and a half years I owned it, I changed the screen about four times. Contrast that experience with Motorola V50 with my experience with Nokia 1110, which I used uninterruptedly for two years before I got fed up and gave it to my last daughter, Athenia. It never for once broke down. If it fell from any height and scattered into five pieces, you just collected the pieces, slot in the battery in its compartment, slide close the battery holder and it jumped back to live. On top of its durability, it doubled as a touch light, a great utility in Nigeria where electricity remains a luxury.

To know how you're really performing, let your customers tell you through surveys. The survey can be through unstructured or structured focus groups, mall intercept opinion surveys, mail questionnaires, or regular consultant conducted opinion polls. The outcome of the surveys should be summarized and subjected to rigorous statistical analysis to get meaning out of them. Unless the surveys are statistically analyzed, you run the danger of drawing wrong conclusions.

Properly analyzed, the survey should reveal gaps where you are falling behind industry's best practice. This will give you an indication of the amount of work you need to do to make further progress in your journey to Excellence. ABB (Asea Brown Boveri) conducts regular on-going customer surveys and takes action anytime their customer satisfaction level falls below 96 per cent. SAS similarly conducted regular on-going customer surveys at the time of Jan Carlzon and took action anytime their customer satisfaction rating fell below 96 per cent. The ultimate aim for conducting surveys is to reduce to the barest minimum your customer sacrifice - the difference between the customers's ideal and what they settle for. I switched from Motorola to Nokia because the sacrifice of owning Motorola and having to shell out N4,000 ($31 at the time) every three or so months to fix the Motorola V50 phone screen was too high. Regular customer survey is a highly cost effective way of finding out the customer's complaints and sentiments about your products and services and the time to begin doing it is today.

Bridge Sixty

HAVE A MYSTERY SHOPPER TELL YOU HOW YOUR STAFF TREAT CUSTOMERS

As the CEO, observe the way your people treat you. Anywhere and everywhere, whether you're going or coming, they treat you with courtesy, sometimes deference, affection, happiness, admiration, excitement, enthusiasm, and sometimes fear. They want to be close to you. Sometimes they fawn. They more or less adore you. To them, you're the center of the universe.

Now, do you ever ask yourself if your people treat or relate to your customers the same way they treat or relate to you? Are they kind, nice, enthusiastic, loving, energetic - everything you want them to be when dealing with the customer? You may want to find out. Reverse your role. Put on a disguise and visit your company as a customer. A branch away from the head office, if you are a bank, for example, may just be the right place to visit. What do you see? Were you treated the same way you're treated as the CEO? Most probably not! You have just played a *mystery shopper* and you can now make your report to the board and decide what action to take.

The *Mystery Shopper* concept is one of the weapons in the multidisciplinary arsenal of approaches world-class organizations use in monitoring and measuring some aspects of their service delivery process. *Mystery shopping* is predicated on the belief that only the customer can give objective information on *the* actual service experience. Mystery Shoppers are individuals assigned the task of posing as customers to collect information concerning their actual experiences.

The M*ystery Shopper* will visit your toilet, observe first hand how your people treat customers, observe your people's telephone manners, mail turnaround time, in fact, everything you need to know about the way customers are treated. What you can find out is only limited by the scope of the brief you give the *mystery shopper.*

Heskett and his colleagues in their **Service Breakthroughs** quote Younkers, a departmental store chain in the US as carrying out 12,000 *mystery shoppings* a year in support of its *Satisfaction Plus* quality and productivity effort. Kotler also quotes many other organizations, including banks, as relying on mystery shopping to monitor where their service delivery chains are breaking down. In Nigeria, many banks and fast food chains use mystery shoppers to monitor their service. When one bank I know began using mystery shoppers, one senior executive reported that it was unbelievable what he saw in the debrief video clips taken from the tiny hidden video camera carried by the mystery shopper.

Mystery shopping together with your other customer surveys will help you decide where to target your service efforts. Now is the time for you to ask a mystery shopper to help you find out how your people treat customers. You can get more information on how to get the services of a certified mystery shopper in Nigeria by sending email enquiries to visionandtalentltd@gmail.com. We recently started carrying out unsolicited mystery shopping in fast food outlets all over Lagos and it's unbelieveable what we discovered. I showed one of the picture shots to the founder of Terra Kulture, Bolanle Austen-Peters, and she nearly threw up. I had to apologise. The shots were from one of the fastest growing fast foods chains in the country. Don't be surprised, even the new generation fast foods are no better.

Bridge Sixty One

DELIVER SERVICE TO THE *STANDARD* YOUR CUSTOMER SETS FOR YOU – NOT YOUR STANDARD

In the late 70s to early 80s, quality was the winning ticket. If you had quality you won. In the US, that was the time when the Malcolm Baldridge National Quality Award came into being. The first organization to win the award was Motorola. That was in 1975. Since then, more than 100 organizations of various sizes and in different industries have won the award. Quality awareness is now all pervasive to the extent that every organization has Quality.

To show that they care about quality, every organization now has one form of quality statement or another. They come in various guises. Some organizations call theirs *Quality Testament*, others have names such as, *Quality Promise, Quality Pact, Quality Creed.* We had earlier quoted the *L.L. Bean Golden Rule.* There is also the *Johnson & Johnson Credo.* In short, these are the quality standards these organizations set for themselves.

It is very critical that you set standards in all aspects of your operation. Standards serve as basis for measurement, for you can't manage quality unless you measure it. Standards are particularly important in people oriented businesses with a high service content, example restaurants, banking, airlines and such like. However, don't be deceived. Standard is of limited value unless it's the customer's standard. The *Standard* is what the customer says it is.

Many executives find it difficult to accept this view point. They say, the customer does not understand this business, why should they set standard for us? Myopia! The essence of the business is to serve the customer so the standard is what the customer says it is. You fight against this notion in vain. If the customer says for instance, the standard for answering the telephone is one ring and you say our standard is 30 seconds that is 5.5 rings. To you, that is excellent. To the customer, 5.5 rings is eternity. The customer will not like you. The customer will ditch you and you will become like Long Term Capital Management, Lehman Brothers, Merryl Lynch, to mention but a few of once great organizations with great history that have all gone under or sold themselves to others for a pittance. Don't forget, its perception that matters, above all else, not fact.

Bridge Sixty Two

HAVE 3-5 SERVICE DIMENSIONS IN WHICH YOU WISH TO BE *THE LEADER*

If you are a secretary, probably the service dimension with the highest payoff for you would be 100 per cent error free word processing (call it typing). That is at the personal or individual level. For a car manufacturer, it would probably be design, days to the market, agency relations, supplier relations, low cost inventory. The banker would probably pursue responsiveness, courteousness, hassles-free account opening procedures, service, least overall cost/income ratio, etc.

Every industry has what management experts call critical success factors. What are the critical success factors in your industry? In short, what can you do, that if you did very well, will have the greatest impact on your entire operations? What can you do to stand out from the also ran. Where are you focusing your effort? Are you trying to be everything to all men? Assuming you are a bank and a potential customer were to ask, where in this neighborhood can I open account hassles-free, would people point to your bank? If not, think again. The same thing goes to every other business. The simpler you make things for the customer, the better.

Bridge Sixty Three

CONSTANTLY MEASURE YOUR CUSTOMER'S PROFITABILITY

Marvin Bower, the founder of McKinsey & Co. was quoted as saying that the primary purpose of business is not profit. If you do it well, he contended, the profits will come. Marvin Bower of course knew because as someone who had set up and managed what is arguably the best consulting business in the world he was well placed to know the key drivers of business success. Now assuming that you have done it well and the profits have come, what strategies are you going to use to ensure you guarantee and sustain those profits?

The key in this regard is to constantly measure your customer's profitability. You see despite your good efforts, only a certain proportion of your customers will account for the bulk of your revenue. This phenomenon is known variously as the Pareto principle or the 80/20 rule. Simply stated, it says that 80 per cent of your profit (outcome) will come from 20 per cent of your customers (efforts). The principle also holds true in other spheres of business. The key therefore is to be able to isolate the top 20 per cent of the customers that are accounting for 80 per cent of your profit and go a further mile to serve them.

There are countless things you can do of which we have mentioned in various other sections of this book. The key is to model whatever you do to produce a net tangible benefit for the customer. Airlines for instance have their frequent-flyer programmes. You too can create your frequent-user programme. It's that simple. These days there are different forms of computer software you can use to construct a database that can help you track who the people using your services are. These systems are quite cheap and within the reach of any medium sized business that is desirous of keeping track of its performance.

Bridge Sixty Four

KNOW, TO THE CUSTOMER, QUALITY MEANS 100 PER CENT CORRECT

Philip Crosby has said "*companies continue to fight the quality battle the old fashioned way, with excuses.*" It's Crosby who handed down the tough standard that the measurement standard must be '*Zero Defects*', and not '*That's close enough*'. Tony Ansell admonishes that, "*while manufactured goods can have a tolerance level, money must be 100 per cent accurate.*" In illustrating, Ansell said a customer would take a very serious offence if for instance he made £1,000 deposit and his banker credited £999.99, to his bank account, a negligible error of just 0.001%. There is nothing like a small error or a little mistake when it comes to customer service. Take the case of the common ruler. If you went to a shop to buy one for your son preparing for WAEC exams and the shop attendant were to tell you a particular ruler was 11.98 inches long, just 0.02 inches short of 12 inches, the length for a standard ruler, you probably wouldn't accept that particular one. Right? You would scout all the shops until you found the one that was 12 inches exactly. Why? After all, your son could still pass his exams even with a ruler that is 10 inches in length! It's something psychological.

Sometimes poor quality can have tragic consequences and result in national calamity as the Space Shuttles Challenger and Columbia disasters of January 28, 1986 and February 1, 2003 respectively epitomized! Till date NASA has not been able to definitively fix the problem that is blamed on the insulation foam tiles. The tiles keep peeling off during lift off so every time a shuttle makes re-entry to earth we all hold our breath. It's time NASA fixed the tiles problem once and for all.

Bridge Sixty Five

CONSTANTLY MEASURE YOUR CUSTOMER'S SATISFACTION LEVEL

Tony Ansell, formerly Head of Quality Assurance, Banking Operations, Midland Bank, in a paper he presented at the 21st Cambridge Seminar of The Chartered Institute of Bankers (now Institute of Financial Services), held at Christ's College, Cambridge, in September 1993 titled **Approaches To Quality Management – Putting It Into Practice At A Local Level**, gave two sets of questions, all ten in number, that you can ask to convince yourself whether your quality programme is really top notch. The first set of questions were concerned with flavour of the month initiatives such as badges with capital 'Q' on them, posters encouraging quality, quality slogans that relate little to everyday actions, short term targets and consultants driven process. The second set of ten questions addressed the very roots of the company and included such things as the amount of time the CEO allocates to quality management, careful auditing of customers' requirements, cost of quality, and measures of error amongst others.

Ansell affirmed that if the answer to a number of the first set of questions was "*yes*", then the organization had a very effective "*cosmetic quality*" programme that may delude senior management into thinking that the company was a "quality company - without having any major effect on *customers* or your profits." Conversely, according to Ansell, if you can answer *yes* to the questions in the second group, you have a "*real quality*" management operation. Quality is a journey and not a destination as those that have started the journey have found out. You cannot really *arrive*.

Bridge Sixty Six

TAKE ACTION ANY TIME YOUR CUSTOMER SATISFACTION RATING FALLS BELOW 100%

At the 1976 Olympics, Nadia Comaneci of Romania scored a perfect 10 on her performance on the un-even bars. Nadia was the first person in the Women's Artistic Gymnastic History to score a perfect 10. Nadia won 3 individual gold medals at the 1976 Olympics in Montreal and 2 more in the 1980 Moscow Olympics. She was a legend in the sport. At those games she received 7 perfect 10s. Nadia was just 14 at the time of her first feat in 1976. When asked how she felt about her feat, she simply said, "nothing". To her it was just the natural thing to do, she couldn't imagine of scoring anything below 10. That is the spirit!

Your *customer satisfaction rating* is the barometer of your standing with your customers. The minimum acceptable score is 100 per cent. Take action immediately your customer satisfaction rating falls below 100 per cent. Many organizations have what they call trigger points below which they take action if their customer satisfaction rating falls. As we highlighted in Bridge *Fifty Nine*, for ABB it was 96 per cent, and for SAS it was also 96 per cent. Ninety six percent looks unforgivingly high, until you look behind the figures. For an airline that carries 2.5 million passengers in a year, 96% means in a typical year 100,000, that is 4%, of those passengers are not happy, much less being delighted. For an airline that carries about 10 million passengers like British Airways, that figure comes to 400,000, enough to fill Maracana stadium four times over. Maracana stadium you may know is one of football's most glamourous stadia in Rio De Janeiro, Brazil!

The story, perhaps apocryphal, is told how IBM requested the Fujitsu Corporation of Japan to manufacture on its behalf some microchips, setting what IBM believed to be a very high standard of no more than "three defective chips per 10,000." When IBM received the chips, it was said, there was an accompanying letter that read in part *"we Japanese do not understand American business practices. However, the three defective parts per 10,000 are enclosed, and are wrapped separately."* To Fujitsu, the standard is 100 per cent correct. To IBM at the time, the standard was, 'that's close enough'.

IBM has come a long way since then. Lou Gerstner, who was head-hunted in 1993 to turn IBM around from the brink of disaster, tells the graphic story of IBM'S long march to freedom in his exhilarating book **Who Says Elephants Can't Dance?** Gerstner revealed that when he first arrived at IBM, he asked, *"What do our customers think about us?"* He requested to see the customer satisfaction data and the reports he got were amazingly positive, while IBM was losing market share in almost every product line. It turned out, Gerstner revealed, that IBM measured customer satisfaction by assigning the task to the sales forces. The sales staff simply picked some of their customers and asked them to complete a survey questionnaire. Of course the sales people picked their best and happiest customers and IBM was getting lots of positive data and fooling itself. Gerstner revealed that IBM was conducting 339 different customer satisfaction surveys and because it used different methodologies, it was impossible to get a single view. Gerstner changed all that. Gerstner emphasized, *''Today we conduct fourteen comprehensive customer surveys, administered by an independent research firm. Names are sourced from external lists and we interview almost 100,000 customers and non-customers every year."* To ensure IBM captures as large a spectrum of their customer universe as possible, the surveys are carried out in fifty five countries employing as much as thirty five languages. IBM's performance is then compared to those of all their major competitors and the information derived therefrom is immediately incorporated into their tactical and strategic plans semiweekly. Any wonder by the time Gerstner stepped down and handed over to the new CEO, Sam Palmisano, on March 1, 2002, IBM's per share price had climbed to $120.96, relative to the lackluster $12.72 it was on March 31, 1993 when he took charge, while revenue grew to $85.9bn in 2001, compared to $64.5bn in 1992.

Do not be deceived by the statistics. When your customer satisfaction rating reads 99 per cent, do not forget the statistics have also somewhat been adjusted for margin of error, and is more likely to be lower than 99 per cent as we humans are always very optimistic when it comes to things like quality or satisfaction that you cannot touch but can only perceive. Don't rely on statistics; ask every customer, are you delighted by the way we serve you and if you don't get 100 per cent unequivocal *yes* answer run helter-skelter in search of what to do. Remember, according to Benjamin Disraeli, "There are three kinds of Lies: Lies, Damn Lies and Statistics."

Bridge Sixty Seven

PURSUE SIX-SIGMA, IN SHORT, PURSUE PERFECTION

It was Jean Riboud of Schlumbeger who once said *"to be excellent is fine, but that is not good enough, the aim is to strive for perfection"*. He was right on target. Excellent companies strive for perfection. When next you come across a Lexus advert, look at it closely, the tag line is *'in pursuit of perfection'*. By now you already know that Lexus is the luxury car division of Toyota. Philip Crosby coined the phrase 'Zero Defects' to emphasize that *being close* is just not good enough. You either have it or you don't.

Quality = 100%.

Tom Peters extols mistakes. Tom even queries the usefulness of Philip Crosby's *'Zero Defect'* approach. My view is, for routine procedural activities, for example, typing letters, answering the phone, counting notes, and the like, the standard must be zero tolerance for mistakes. However, for complex creative endeavours such as designing a new car, writing new software and the like, mistakes are inevitable, for such endeavours are a matter of trial and error. Of course *'bold failures'*, as Tom characterizes gigantic efforts, are permitted and even welcomed as far as the drive for perfection is concerned for we cannot really make omelet without breaking an egg.

You make a very big mistake when you measure your error rate in percentage terms. Take a typical bank. If the bank has 100,000 customers, and is achieving 99 per cent error-free dispatch of account statements to its customers, it means every month at least 1,000 customers wont get their account statement. The bank may report in its in-house magazine that it is top dog in quality and points at the 99 per cent achievement level in dispatching account statements. But in reality, the bank has 1,000 unhappy customers just on this score (account statement delivery) alone. As the number of steps in a process increases, the nonconformance rate increases exponentially. As Adedeji B. Badiru and Babatunde J. Ayeni point out in their **Practitioner's Guide to Quality and Process Improvement**, "*a process that is 99 per cent perfect will produce 10,000 defects per million parts. The total yield (number of non-defective units) from a process is determined by a combination of the performance levels of all the steps making up the process*". According to the authors, as the number of steps in a process increases, the number of defects increases exponentially. For instance if a process has 20 steps all of which are 98% perfect, then the overall process performance will be only *66.7608%*. "*Thus, the process will produce 332,392 defects per million parts,*" according to the authors.

We must aim at 100 per cent quality because doing otherwise leads to chronic wastage as we have seen. Companies with world class quality allow for no more than 3.4 defects per million parts in manufactured goods or 3.4 mistakes per million activities in a service operation. Adedeji B. Badiru is Associate Professor, School of Industrial Engineering, University of Oklahoma, and Babatunde J. Ayeni is Statistical Specialist, 3M Information Technology, Statistical Consulting Dept., St. Paul, Minnesota. They two well respected experts point out that, "*A process will need to be 99.99966 per cent perfect in order to produce only 3.4 defects per million.*" This is the so called the six-sigma approach to quality. Implemented by companies such as Motorola's, GE and other worldclass companies, six-sigma in reality pushes for perfection. The approach uses statistical methods to find problems that cause defects. Six-sigma means six standard deviations from a statistical performance average. The approach helps to set a quality standard and provides a mechanism for striving to reach the goal. In effect, Badiru and Ayeni posit, the six-sigma process means '*changing the way people do things so as to minimize the potential for defects.*' That probably informs Lexus' tag line, *In Pursuit of Perfection*. Typical of Toyota, they will never tell you they are pursuing six-sigma in contrast to Motorola. I wonder why Motorola has not been able to use six-sigma to eliminate the problem that caused the screen of their V50 GSM phones (now phased out) to freeze and turn black every 90 days or so! I recounted my experience with the V50 in Bridge Fifty Nine. Motorola's 'best' phone according to Fortune was the *RAZR* but I didn't fancy it very much as I was not enamored to the sound, 'Hello Moto!', that came with new Motorola phones. Ironically, since RAZR, nothing *hot* has come out of Motorola's stable while Nokia keeps churning out new toys.

PART 5

MINING IDEAS EVERYWHERE

Bridge Sixty Eight

TEST YOUR NEW IDEAS WITH THE CUSTOMER

Sometimes you have a flash of inspiration and your new product idea becomes an instant hit. The market beckons and with little or no effort, you make tons of money. However, things don't always work out this way. Sometimes you have to toil and sweat to get your product to the market. With a little luck and heavy advertising, the market may come to accept your product.

If your new product offering is really for the customer, it makes sense to test the new product with the customer before you embark on serious production. You risk massive and spectacular failure if you don't. The spectacular failure in the late 1970s of the Wendy Osimov's *flying car*, with doors that opened vertically sky-wards readily comes to mind in this regard. Osimov, whose factory was located in Ireland had planned to sell 500,000 cars, however, in the end, he sold only 200 cars and his venture flopped.

Honda's 50cc motor cycle had a happier ending. After making their heavy 500cc, 200cc and other big models, Honda's salesmen went on 50cc models to market the heavy models. The salesmen extolled the virtues of the heavy models and described how exhilarating the ride on them was. But to the salesmen's utter consternation, their target customers demanded the light 50cc models they were riding. This was in India. First the salesmen refused to believe what they were hearing. Eventually, they had no choice but to listen and the light 50cc Honda motorcycle has come to become the biggest selling motorcycle in the world.

Then there is the funny story of the Post-It Notes. Invented almost by accident by Arthur Fry, Post-It Notes have become one of the greatest selling products of all time. After 3M team made the first Post-It Notes, rather than wait for marketing people to push the product, they used it to send hand written notes to their colleagues in other depts. 3M CEO used Post-It Notes to write short messages to his colleagues in other corporations. The secretary to 3M's boss was soon to be inundated with demands from within and outside the company about "those little yellow *sticky notes* the CEO writes on". The 3M Post-it Note has been a run-away success since they first rolled off the conveyor belt in Minnesota in 1971. The 3M people learnt to test their ideas with the customer.

Bridge Sixty Nine

KNOW THE BEST IDEAS WILL COME FROM THE CUSTOMER

Bridge Sixty Nine *know the best ideas will come from the customer* is about getting attuned to what the customer is saying. You must listen hard not only to hear what the customer is saying but also to understand the hidden message in what he is saying. More often than not, the customer will not tell you anything directly, but his actions will point you to his thinking. It is then left for you to uncover the unspoken message.

Let me give you an example. Close to 100 years, Lever Brothers (Unilever) and Paterson Zachonis (PZ) were the only makers of detergent in Nigeria. Omo, Surf and Elephant are their brands. Together they controlled 100% of the market for detergents. Omo and Elephant for 40 years came in standard 450gm carton packs. Because of their prices, which hovered around N120 per pack at some point, most low income households were unable to afford them. Sensing this, petty traders (the mallams – security guards for the elite and nouveau riche who also do petty trading to augment their meager pay) started to repack the product in 2gm, 5gm and 10gm transparent nylon sachets and retail them at between N0.5 to N5 apiece depending on the area.. This was a pointer to Lever Brothers and PZ to take action, but for many years Lever and PZ ignored the market signal.

Then some importers with bright ideas flew to Indonesia and made arrangement for 10gm well packaged detergents. That was the genesis of *Klin,* the beautifully scented detergent from Indonesia sold in beautifully packaged 10 gm sachets. Before long Procter & Gamble saw the opportunity and jumped into the fray by launching *Ariel* in 20 gm sachets. Before Lever Brothers and PZ could wake up from their slumber they had lost 50% of the market for detergents to P & G, which was barely seven years old in Nigeria in 1998. Today Lever and PZ produce the 5gm and10gm sachets but they hardly control 35% of the market, a sharp fall from the 100% share they once collectively controlled with insensitive impunity.

Sony, the Japanese electronics giant is in the forefront of innovation. After observing that to listen to music while on the go, youths on both sides of the Atlantic carried heavy stereo sets on their shoulders in the street, Sony concluded the youth were trying to tell them something. And that is how the Sony Walkman was born. Late Akio Morita, the co-founder of Sony, described how Sony engineers kicked against the whole idea. The engineers argued that since the Walkman had no recording capacity it would not fly. A visionary that he was, Morita saw what the engineers could not see. John Nathan in his **Sony, The Private Life,** said Morita ordered the production of 30,000 units and announced that he would resign as chairman if the 30,000 units fell to sell. In the end, the Walkman sold more than 500,000 units within the first one year. From the middle of September, 1979, just two and half months after the product was launched, and for the rest of the year, production capacity had to be doubled and tripled every month. Morita, the marketing legend that he was, knew the best ideas always come from the customer.

The same thing goes to the fortuitous invention of Post-It Notes by 3M we earlier highlighted in Bridge Sixty Eight. After the paper he used as a page marker repeatedly fell off during a choir practice, Arthur Fry, the 3M scientist who invented Post-It Notes, who was also a chorister, decided he had to do something about his dilemma. He did and that is how the Post-it Note was born. In this instance Arthur Fry was the customer; he saw a need and took steps to address the need.

Bridge Seventy

IF YOU NEED A SECOND OPINION ASK THE CUSTOMER

Since the inception of the modern industrial corporation over 150 years ago, organizations have always made laws to suit themselves. They arbitrarily fix their opening and closing hours, they fix the time they can receive visitors and so on. Take the case of opening hours in banks. Before banks saw the light, they opened from 8am to 3.30pm on Mondays and 8am to 1.30pm on Tuesdays to Fridays. The opinion of the customer counted for nothing. Not that people had no need for banking services after 3.30pm on Mondays or 1.30pm on other days. No more. The 'new generation' banks quickly read the public mood and committed to opening from 8am to 5pm Monday to Friday and before long they added Saturday banking to the bargain and they were handsomely rewarded by the customers. The old generation banks saw the hand writing on the wall and quickly followed suit. The customer is happier for it. The same scenario played out when GSM telephony first debutted in Nigeria. While customers clamoured for per second billing, the front runners (MTN and Econet (now Zain)) said per second billing was not feasible and stuck to per minute billing. So if you made a call for 25 seconds you paid one minute rate. Before you could say miracle, GloMobile came along and announced per second billing, and overnight all the other networks ate their words and jumped into the fray.

Most forward looking organizations seek the opinion of their *partners* before deciding anything. They put the convenience of the customer ahead of their internal convenience. However, this is not the case with government ministries Nigeria. We had earlier talked about the Ministry of Education and its agencies (WAEC- West African Examination Council, JAMB-Joint Admission & Matriculation Board, NUC-National Universities Commission), other government agencies such as NITEL (Nigeria Telecoms Ltd. - nothing has happened there since it was privatized or sold to Transcorp in 2004 or so), and PHCN in Bridge Six. All policies of MOE and its agencies as we pointed out seem designed to inflict the maximum amount of injury, damage, hardship, pain and inconvenience to its customers - the millions of students that sit for their exams across the country yearly, and their parents. From sale of their forms to obtaining exam number, and getting of exam result, the story is the same; hardship is the order of the day.

Would it not be better for MOE and its agencies to actively seek the opinion of its customers to establish the most convenient way to execute its programmes? JAMB and WAEC cannot know what is best for the students unless they go out and ask the students and their guardians. In other words, these agencies must look at things from the outside-in, as Peter Drucker puts it. It is only by so doing they can come to understand if their policies are succeeding or failing.

True WAEC and JAMB have taken steps to create websites and institute on-line registration. At their various websites, exam candidates can check their exam centers, which is well and good. Sadly, this websites are notorious for downtime and slow running. Sometimes you need a whole day to get simple information. WAEC and JAMB need to constantly monitor their websites and carry out upgrades to ensure their speed is up to scratch. It was laughable hearing JAMB spokesman blaming candidates for logging on at the same time a few days to the exam whereas they could have logged on a week earlier. JAMB you're wrong. Upgrade your website and let candidate be able to log in at anytime, get the information they want and move on.

Nigeria Immigration Services is another bad website. The website is so poorly designed you may spend a whole day roaming about, doing trial and error and still end up not knowing what to do. It took me over one week to 'master' the site. If you seek the assistance of a Nigeria Immigration Services official, the best you'll get is a sympathetic advice to "try a business centre." Nigeria Immigration Services please upgrade your website, make it more customer-friendly and make it possible for your customers to be able to get refund if they apply for the wrong passport. I for one applied for passport renewal as directed by an Assistant Comptroller of Immigration only to be told after I'd paid on-line that what I needed was passport re-issue. After fooling around on the website for over two weeks, a sympathetic officer told me I should not waste my time with a re-issue as the website had a defect, I should just go ahead and apply for a fresh passport. As for refund of the N2,600 renewal fees I had earlier paid he told me I should just forget about it as no one in their ranks had the information on how to process refund for fees paid on-line. There is no instruction in the website how to get refund. I'm still hoping the Comptroller General of Nigeria Immigration Services will authorize a refund before it becomes statute barred.

It always pays to seek a second opinion from the customer. Tom Peters and Nancy Austin give copious examples of companies that live for the customer. One of them is Stew Leonard's, then a one-store dairy operation at Norwalk, Connecticut. In the PBS film, **In Search of Excellence,** Stew Leonard Jr. who runs the shop with his father recalls that they used to sell fish in their store already 'plastic-wrapped', and in one of their customer-focus group meetings a lady complained "*I don't like your fish because it's not fresh.*" Stew Leonard Jr. said, "*so what we did was to set up a fish bar with ice in it. Now there's wrapped fish in one place, but some people like to buy it fresh right off the ice.*" That simple action, wait for it, resulted in a doubling of store's sales volume to 30,000 pounds as against 15,000 pounds. Just one action. The story is told of an elderly lady who passed away and requested that her most cherished personal effects be buried inside a Stew Leonard's shopping bag within her casket. Her relatives stated that Stew Leonard's was her favorite shopping place. Any wonder Stew Leonard's sold more than 10 times the industry average and grossed $85million from a single store at the time this story was told way back in 1985. Stew Leonard's as we mentioned earlier in 1992 entered the Guinness Book of World Records for the highest sales per square foot of space. Contrast Stew Leonard's' approach with most companies that take every customer's suggestion or feed back as an affront. The typical defensive response is always something to the effect that the customer is the only one complaining. How wrong!

Bridge Seventy One

DON'T TAKE THE CUSTOMER OUT FOR *LUNCH* UNLESS YOU HAVE A NEW IDEA TO SHARE

Ever since ancient times, people have always tried to be nice to other people who have done them a favor. In the corporate world, this takes different forms. The most popular ways of expressing "gratitude" include sending seasonal greeting cards, specially made hampers and other designer gift items, plagues, and the like. Another thing that is rapidly gaining in popularity is the taking of people out for lunch. This is now common practice, especially in big corporations.

Stop to think about it, do you need to take your customer out for lunch? What's the purpose at the heart of it all? Is it a polite way of saying thank you for what you have done for me lately, or an indirect way of bribing someone? Well, all through this book we have emphasized the need to build relationships, to construct bridges to the customer's heart, to add value, to build loyalty and trust. If lunch is one of the things you like doing, then do it if it'll strengthen the existing bonds between you and your customer. Let the lunch be for a purpose. Let lunch be the time when you don't only tell the customer you care, but let it be an occasion when you share new ideas with the customer, when you draw the customer's attention to new opportunities he may not be aware of. Arrange the whole lunch in such a way that the customer looks forward to it.

But beware. A fine line has to be drawn between lunch for the purpose of relationship building and that which aims to corrupt the customer. The Salt Lake City 2002 winter Olympics scandal readily comes to mind. It is on record as can be gleaned from internet records and graphically captured in the Salt Lake City Organizing Committee (SLCOC) website that while bidding for the games organizers *"spent millions on perks for IOC officials including all-expense-paid ski trips, thirteen scholarships, Super Bowl trips, and plastic surgery."* It did not stop there. The website further revealed that "*IOC members were given deals on real estate, and their family members were given jobs. It is also rumored that professional 'escorts' may have been provided to some visiting delegates to Salt Lake City. More controversially cash bribes may have been employed.*"

The scandal came to light aound December 10, 1998, when Swiss IOC member , Marc Hodler, head of the coordination committee overseeing the organization of the 2002 accused some of their members of taking bribes. The IOC, US Olympic Committee and SLOC immediately started looking into the matter and before long the US Department of Justice filed a total of fifteen bribery and fraud charges against the two key members of SLOC mentioned in the scandal. As a result of the scandal it is estimated that at least ten members of the IOC were expelled and another ten were sanctioned. According to internet sources, such action (expulsion) had never taken place before in the more than 100 year history of IOC. We have gone to this length to draw a line between attempts at bribery and straight forward business luncheon.

Bribing for business is akin to doping enroute to an Olympic gold medal. Remember Ben (Bullet) Johnson of Canada, who ran the 100 meters dash in 9.8 seconds, the fastest 100 meters in Olympic history only to be disgraced when he failed a drug test. His Gold Medal was retrieved and awarded to Carl Lewis, the second place winner. Early in October 2007, Marion Jones, who for 10 years consistently denied ever taking performance enhancing drugs, finally pleaded guilty to doping and is to forfeit the 5 gold medals she won at the Sydney Olympics and is to in addition serve a minimum of 6 months behind bars! In fact in the second week of March 2008, she started her six months jail term and will have the tag ex-convict as part of her name for the rest of her life. What a sad end to what otherwise would have been a glorious career if the temptation to cut corners had been resisted.

For the small business, elaborate entertainment of customers may not be a viable proposition but it can be done. If you are a small business, then your customers will equally be people of average means. You don't have to take your customer to overly expensive restaurants. The customer will be embarrassed if you did that and may even be suspecting you're trying to bribe him. In the lunch thing, it's the spirit behind it that's important. Be useful to the customer. Be creative. Before we launched a new computer training program years back in the now defunct consultancy and finance house subsidiary of the then Nigerian Agricultural and Cooperative Bank Ltd. (NACB) (now Bank of Agriculture-BOA), in Kaduna, we invited several CEOs of the top companies in the town for lunch at 6-0-J Restaurant along Ahmadu Bello Way. While we expected 20 guests, over 50 turned up for the "training program unveiling carnival" that included presentation by the GM, late D. O. A. Adelana, and a three-course meal that included catfish pepper soup! The attendees wondered how we would make money. But computer awareness was the in-thing. In the weeks following the program unveiling event, even NACB, our parent company, sent over 60 of its staff to be trained. Needless to say we made money before the 1993 'June 12' upheaval and its aftermath resulted in the collapse of the over 1,000 finance houses in the country and the eventual demise of NACB-CFC. In conclusion, if you have no new ideas to share, do not invite the customer out for lunch.

Bridge Seventy Two

PICK THE BRAIN OF YOUR CUSTOMERS

Ten heads are better than one. Right! Ever since the industrial revolution, companies have tended to structure to ensure maximum comfort of their staff. The same goes to the policies, rules and procedures they adopt. Though meant to guide their internal working arrangements, the effect of their policies and rules always invariably impact negatively on their customers. Samples:

a)   No refund after payment (shops/supermarkets)
b)   Vehicles are parked at owners' risk (hotels, banks)
c)   Cash must be counted at the counter (banks)
d)   No visitors allowed during office hours or between 12 and 2pm

We can go on and on. Recall Bridge Seventy *If You Need a Second Opinion Ask the Customer*. You cannot know how negative (call that obnoxious) a policy is until you put yourself in the customer's shoes. To find out though, ask the customer, and most will be glad to tell you the areas that need improvement or change. The customer, mark you, is the best and cheapest source of information you'll ever get. You know why? Unlike the consultant, he will not charge you for giving you useful suggestions and ideas.

There are many ways you can pick the brain of the customer. One simple way is to listen to all the comments he makes while he's in your premises. Take down the comments and ask yourself soul searching questions and follow the customer's lead. You can equally invite the customer formally to make suggestions how you can improve your service. How you go about this and what name you call the process is not really material. You can call it focus group; customer roundtable or forum; search group; rescue group and so on. As we said the name is not important. The important thing is your willingness to listen and the courage to go along with the suggested solutions. You can also use various forms of interviews. Of course, there also is the traditional suggestion box. But remember, nobody ever remembers to open the suggestions box. Typically, the suggestion box lacks urgency and no one ever remembers who keeps the key! You can go ahead and keep a suggestion box but know its shortcomings and find creative ways to overcome it. You can decide to pay people for every suggestion that leads to cost savings or generates revenue!

Interpret your findings with care. Beware of statistics. Not that statistics have no place, they do, but as far as the customer is concerned, perception is more important than logic. Let the customers know their suggestions are valued, appreciated and welcome and they will tell you everything. Implement accepted suggestions boldly. Thank the customer that suggested the idea.

Toyota collects customer information in two ways: through its *Customer Assistance Centers* (CAC) and through *Customer Satisfaction Surveys*. Each year, 40 full-time people in the CAC handle some 300,000 customer calls and assist customers with problems or concerns. Customers use 800 toll-free numbers. Toyota says when customers know we're only a phone call away, they feel the company really cares about their satisfaction.

Toyota carried the same zeal over to Lexus. Lexus' success owes as much to Toyota's ingenuity as to customers suggestions. It is said that when Toyota wanted to initiate the Lexus project it sent out detailed questionnaires and interviewed over 5,000 luxury car owners all over the US on what they meant by luxury and excellence. Toyota engineers carefully translated the lay man's language into engineering specifications using the Taguchi techniques. Toyota's ultimate aim was to challenge GM and Mercedes in the upper end segment of the auto market having prevailed at the lower and middle segments with brands such as Corolla, Corona, Avensis, Camry and Crown. Before Lexus, Honda Acura was the only Japanese car that made any meaningful inroad into the middle-to-upper end of the market. Even though Toyota Crown targeted the upper end, the name 'Toyota' was seen as limiting. Toyota was associated with small economy cars. The Lexus project was about luxury and excellence. The Lexus as we earlier stated is advertised with the tag line *the Pursuit of Perfection*.

To effectively position the new model, and decisively distinguish it from Toyota, the company chose the name Lexus and rather than locate the Lexus plant in Japan, it located it in California, the state with the largest concentration of luxury cars in the US.

It was a superb strategy, flawlessly executed to the minutest detail. Lexus engineers successfully eliminated all idling noise from the Lexus until it became the quietest car in the world. When Lexus hit the market it was an instant success. In one of its early adverts, to demonstrate how quiet the Lexus engine was, the Lexus bonnet was opened and a glass of water was placed on the engine. A glass of water was placed also on a Mercedes engine. The two cars were started. While the water in the glass on the Mercedes engine could be seen shaking, that on the Lexus engine did not move. The message was clear. Lexus engine is super quiet. Any wonder, since 1992, Lexus has won Motoring Magazine's 'Best *Car*' for 8 years in a row. The Lexus had arrived and was aggressively taking market share away from Mercedes, which in the meantime had its attention diverted to fixing problems at Chrysler. That is the power of the Bridge, Pick the Brains of your Customers.

Bridge Seventy Three

BORROW IDEAS FROM OTHER INDUSTRIES TO IMPROVE YOUR BUSINESS

How do you feel when your bank addresses you as a number and a color? Is it exhilarating when the bank teller shouts at the top of her voice, number twenty two green, or number six blue or whatever number and color combination they assigned to you? Nigeria's top old generation banks, the so called big three - First Bank, Union Bank and United Bank for Africa - were using this archaic system in most of their branches until very recently.

Since these banks had been using this system for so many years, everybody had come to accept that it was the only system under the sun but as we now know, it wasn't. The banks had simply allowed their collective creativity to go to sleep. The thing is, nobody ever questioned *the way we do things around here*. Over the long haul, when this type of culture permeates the organization, rot starts to set in and before you know it the organization is on a continuous downward slide into irrelevance. And that is exactly what happened to the big three as far as we know, until very recently. In the case of UBA, a new management team led by the charismatic go-getter Tony Elumelu took over and great things have been happening there very lately. UBA has so changed that today it's amongst the employers of choice for most bankers. As for FBN, it is on the critical lap of its Century 2 Project which seeks to transform the bank into Africa's #1 bank and a global player to be reckoned with. Its 2007 public offer was massively (some say as much as 550 times) oversubscribed, itself a massive vote of confidence on the bank's long term prospect. FBN is now restructuring massively. In a recent advert, it boasted, *"We are the first organization in Nigeria to achieve the Information Security Management System ISO/IEC 27001:2005 Certification. This means our customers have one more reason to rely on us for dependable financial services. Proof that we are truly the first."* Whether the ambition to dominate the Africa's financial landscape will be realized only time will tell. In the 2009 edition of Bridges, we specifically said the following about Union Bank of Nigeria Plc. "The *ever-unchanging* UBN, with the quiet achiever and unassuming Barth Ebong at the helm has lately begun to stir." We then went on to talk about its Registrars department as there was not much to say about the main bank. I said, "I was mildly surprised when I visited UBN Registrars at No. 2 Burma Road, Apapa, in Nov. 2007 and everything was spick and span. I'd seen my name in Nestle's unclaimed dividend list and I'd gone to sort things out and I was blown away by what I saw there. UBN Registrars used advanced electronic scheduling system to assign clients to the Registrars (frontline staff) and everything worked so beautifully. I traced the supplier of the equipment to Ikeja. The supplier, when contacted, said he buys the system from Switzerland and supplies to banks and other financial institutions." I then concluded by saying, "but very sincerely, the big three still have a long way to go. Their responsiveness still leaves much to be desired. The signage can do with retouching and tweaking in the case of UBN. In all, the first steps have been taken and as the Zeniths, Diamonds and GTs power along, there is no doubt the big three will feel the heat and ginger their pace." Unfortunately for UBN, the pace was too slow and the bank was taken over along with four other banks, by the Central Bank of Nigeria, and the entire board sacked. More on UBN in my new book *The God's of Quality Strike Back*, due out later in 2011.

It took Nigeria's big three banks more than three decades to change the number and colour combination, but in the case of Carl Sewell, the Cadillac Czar, he took immediate action. He borrowed ideas from other industries to improve his car dealership. He realized that the system of blaring customer's names over a loudspeaker was meant for identifying animals in the zoo. Carl Sewell in his **Customers for Life** (written with Paul Brown) confessed, *"One of the things I hate about car dealerships is that they always have loudspeakers blaring the name of someone somebody is trying to find. It's annoying and unprofessional, but I didn't know what to do about it until I wandered into a pizza place."* When an industry is developing, more often than not, the players closely watch what each other is doing and over time other players start copying what the dominant player does and before long the dominant player's methods becomes *'the standards'*. New entrants take to these standards. Amazingly these standards can endure for decades on end until an unheralded upstart comes from nowhere to upturn the applecart. For instance blaring someones name was *'the standard'* in car dealerships until Carl Sewell Village Cadillac came along. Carl Sewell said he didn't like 'the standard' but he didn't know what to do until he ventured into Chuck E. Cheese – the pizza chain with roudy singing animals, rides, Nitendo games and all one not. With children playing games, screaming, and running all over the place, you would think fulfilling orders after customers buy pizza would be a herculean task with numbers blared over loud speakers. This is how Chuck E. Cheese solves the problem. They give you a number when you place an order just as Barcelos does here in Nigeria and you can go and have fun. When an order is ready a sweet sounding chime goes off and the number of the customer whose pizza is ready is displayed on TV monitors they have all over the place. You only have to look at the TV monitor when you hear the chime and when you see your number you go and collect your pizza. No shouting 'Paul Cyril come over your pizza is ready'! No milling around the service counter. No ansiety someone else will take my pizza.

Carl Sewell said when he observed the way Chuck E. Cheese handled the pizza service he quickly took the idea and implemented in his dealership with a few modifications. Unlike before when loud speakers and microphones used to blare all day instructing customer service reps to go to the parking lot to bring the customer's car that was ready around, now the cashier loggs the information in a computer and same is displayed on TV monitors. The customer service rep that first sees the information on the TV monitor logs in and informs the cashier that he'll go for the car. No more blaring on the microphone *'Please bring up car number 473.'* No more delays, no more customer's complains on this score. Carl Sewell elatedly concluded *"With the new system, there are no loudspeaker announcements, and we always know whether or not the car is on the way up. More important, the average time of delivering the car to the customer has been cut from six minutes to two. All of these improvements can be traced directly back to our visit to the local pizza place."* That's the power of the Bridge: Borrow ideas from other industries to improve your business. Waiting in the line for six minutes in a bank to encash a check, or airline counter to buy a ticket or hospital waiting room to see a doctor can seem like eternity in our nanoseconds globalising world. Imagine cutting those minutes from six to two!

Bridge Seventy Four

CONSTANTLY DREAM UP NEW IDEAS TO SATISFY THE CUSTOMER

Bridge Seventy Four is about letting your imagination fly, it's about letting your people go, it's about deep rooted creativity, innovation and initiative. The thing you should know is that there is no formula or off-the-shelf tool-kit that tells you how you should handle the myriad of situations that you will come across in a typical day at work. No business school will teach you how to handle all situations in the book.

Tom Associates, the Anthony Village, Lagos, based trainers on the 13 of January every year since 1995 organises *Trainers' Clinic* for all training managers in the country. During the Clinic, Tom Associates organises a mini book fair for the participating training managers; participants are also addressed by well selected facilitators on topical issues. At the end sumptuous meals are served all at Tom Associate's expense, as the clinic is free. The clinic affords the company the opportunity to network with key training decision makers and training gate keepers, it affords them the outlet to apprise trainers of their training plans and current training initiatives for the current year and finally affords the company a window to *listen in* and obtain first hand information on what the participating organizations are up to as far as training is concerned. In effect Tom Associates is at least one leg up when it goes on a return visit to the participating organizations. Tom Associates also sends to every organization on the Nigeria telephone directory its monthly newsletter *Interface*. The firm believes these efforts will assure it a growing market share in the years ahead and judged by its growing market share there is no doubt the efforts are yielding bountiful dividends.

Tom Associates in 2010 launched another initiative, the Leadership Development Initiative, where men of honour and good standing are invited to address invited guests, all aimed at developing leadership at all levels in the country. In 2010 Dr. Christopher Kolade, Nigeria's former High Commissioner to the United Kingdom addressed guests on the topic '**Let The Real Leaders Stand Up''.** I was honoured to be invited and had another previledge to meet Dr. Kolade, who not only imparted us his wisdom, he inspired us not to lose faith in our nation. Tom Associates constantly dreams up ideas to satisfy its customers and so can you.

PART 6

TURNING CUSTOMERS' COMPLAINTS INTO GOLD MINES

Bridge Seventy Five

ENCOURAGE YOUR CUSTOMERS TO COMPLAIN ABOUT YOUR SERVICE

The more complaining customers you have the better. Encourage your customers to complain. Complain signals that the customer is on your side and is taking an active interest in the way you're serving her. The day the customer stops complaining you're finished because that means she has reached the limit of her tolerance. When the customer stops complaining it means she has given up on you. The customer will stop complaining when she notices that her complaints do not result in any noticeable improvement on your part. She will stop complaining when she notices that you are not taking steps to correct what she is complaining about. She will stop complaining when she senses that you are indifferent to her plight. She will stop complaining when she senses that you resent her complaints.

Many things under the sun can lead to complaints. In the case of a bank, it could be long queues, it could be illegible figures in the monthly statement, it could be monthly statement that is late in coming, it could be overcharges, and it could be your refusing a facility. The list is endless. The important thing is that you should encourage the customer to complain. By complaining the customer is rendering indirect consultancy services to you by pointing out areas where you're failing. Complaints should be treated as God sent.

Most organizations react negatively to customer's complaints. More often than not, companies are defensive or outright resentful towards complaints. Some companies will accuse the customer of being ungrateful; some will 'educate' the customer how to adjust to the way the company renders service. Some companies even go to the extent of telling complaining customers they are not welcome. These are the most foolish ones. The wise companies behave differently. They encourage the customer to complain and how they do this is the subject of the next Bridge *Inform Your Customers Where to Write or Call to Complain.*

Bridge Seventy Six

INFORM YOUR CUSTOMERS WHERE TO WRITE OR CALL TO COMPLAIN

Encouraging the customer to complain is simple in theory but difficult in practice. You see as human beings, we don't like being told our service stinks. But we have to be willing to listen to that by actively encouraging the customer to complain. You encourage the customer to complain by creating avenues for customer complaints.

The best time to encourage the customer to complain is at the beginning of the relationship. There should be a formal relationship letter in which you let the customer know to whom to complain to in case you're not living up to expectation in your service delivery. Let the customer know where to write to or which number to call in case complaining directly to a designated person is not convenient. Let the customer know his complaints will be welcome and that all complaints will be investigated. When the customer does complain, let him know the exact action you are taking to ensure what he is complaining about will not arise in the future.

Most companies encourage their customers to complain by having toll free numbers to call to lodge complaints. However, very few have a system in place to communicate back to the customers the action they are taking to resolve their complaints. Unless you have such a system the customer will doubt your sincerity.

Monitoring complaints in the course of the relationship requires full time commitment. Normally, all staff, especially frontline staff should be required to log all customer complaints they are aware of, indicating the name of the customer, the time, what the complaint was about, and what actually happened. All complaints should be investigated immediately and the customer should be written to within a few hours of a complaint being logged. A customer receiving such a letter will become convinced that you are serious about customer care. Investigating customer complaints does not mean you look for scapegoats amongst your staff to punish. It means you look at your service delivery system to strengthen the weak links. W. Edward Deming the *father* of total quality had said that 90% of problems stem from the system. Blaming a staff is easier than changing your system, which can be inconvenient for some people. But blaming a staff won't solve the problem.

The ultimate in encouraging customer complaints is to pay every customer who complains a token amount for bringing a problem to your notice. The amount could be N1,000 (about $7) or any amount you deem will motivate people to complain. The amount is not important. What is of significance is that you're paying. A customer who receives your letter acknowledging her complaint and a N1,000 cheque for bringing a problem to your attention will be touched by your action and may well become a partner with you in finding solutions for the initial complaint.

Bridge Seventy Seven

READ ALL YOUR CUSTOMERS' COMPLAINT LETTERS

Encouraging your customers to complain is one thing and the easy part. Taking action on the complaints is quite another thing. The first step towards taking action on customer complaints is to read all complaint letters. In reading the letter, you should go behind the words to comprehend the feeling. You should seek to understand those things the customer did not really say.

Complaints letters should be read by somebody high in the management hierarchy. Ideally, this should be the Customer Satisfaction Director. Also she is the one who should decide, after consultation with the other individuals who will be affected by her decision, what steps to take to resolve problems mentioned in customers letters. At the same time, a Customer Champion Manager - staff specifically dedicated to following through to the ultimate resolution the decisions taken on every issue highlighted in customer complaint letters - should be appointed to assist the director. You may even set up a unit with the sole responsibility of monitoring, tracking and resolving complaints. It is only when such a unit is put in place will there be a reasonable chance of resolving customer problems satisfactorily. Most companies don't have such systems in place; rather they approach customer complaints in a reactive manner by setting up bureaucratic committees or directing their inspection unit to 'review the merit' of such complaints and make 'appropriate' (call that jaundiced) recommendations. Invariably, such an approach results in *we* versus *them* fire brigade exercise or a reactive witch hunting merry-go-round that seeks to find who did what wrong, rather than an objective assessment of what parts of the systems are failing. Most often than not, the problem remains unresolved as inspectors do not like to upturn the apple cart by telling management the system stinks since they are part of management. Inspection reports always focus on people that did things wrong and the punishment that should be meted out rather than things that went wrong and the system that should be reengineered or streamlined or simply eliminated.

Bridge Seventy Eight

PUBLISH ALL YOUR CUSTOMERS' COMPLAINTS LETTERS

Customer complaints are God-sent opportunities for you to know what is happening in your company as regards some aspects of your service. They draw your attention to where you're coming on strong and where you're failing. Encourage customers to complain, reward them for their complaints, take action on the complaints and afterwards publicize everything. Use every available media to talk about what your customer complained about, the actions that your company took or is taking, the people that were involved and what the customer's reaction was afterwards.

Knowing the customer's reaction is very vital. The customer feedback is part of the so called 360-degree assessment of your performance. Unless the customer expresses satisfaction, and even delight, with the steps you have taken, to him, nothing has really changed. Sometimes there is no one right answer or solution to a problem. Take the case of the customer that complains that the central air-conditioning system at the reception area is too cold. Do you switch off the air-conditioning system? Do you serve the customer coffee? Do you relocate the reception to another area? All are good questions but no easy answer? Ultimately what is required is a constant tinkering with the system. You have to try different combinations, in a trial and error fashion until you hit the right combination.

In Bridge Six I recounted my ordeal with NICON on my *prosperity plan* that matured but took NICON ages to pay up. After the policy matured, as I'd recounted, I expected to be paid within a week from the Kaduna office that was administering the policy. But the Kaduna office said no, explaining that the payment had to come from the head office, which is quite normal as far as insurance matters are concerned. But that was the end of everything normal about the whole episode and the beginning of the long waiting game. To cut a long story short, the waiting lasted more than six months. I had to write to the CEO of NICON and the company wrote to apologize for the delay and assured me I would receive the payment within 'a few days'. The few days actually came to 35 days.

Now tell me is that service? As I asked rhetorically earlier, if it took me, the policy holder and beneficiary, more than six months to get paid, how many months do you think it would have taken my next-of-kin if I had died? Well I didn't die and I did what any rational man would have done, I walked away, and abandoned the policy losing N1,500 in 1993 money in the process. Till date, fifteen years on, NICON, the biggest insurance company in West Africa has not written to find out why I abandoned the policy. No staff of the company has visited me to say, hey Paul, our prosperity plan is great, and why are you behind in your premiums? NICON does not read its customer complaint letters and hence misses valuable opportunities to become a great company! In the 2009 edition we wrote "NICON today is fighting a life and death battle for survival as the Committee that was set up by the Federal Ministry of Finance to investigate the scandal that trailed the process of recapitalization of insurance companies has recommended its certificate be withdrawn. The new owner, Alhaji Jimoh Ibrahim, has gone to court, quickly followed by the Federal Government taking over the company and predictably now suing for out of court settlement. A total mess you would say but that is the steep price poorly run companies pay when the market place exacts its price. Of course the matter will be settled and NICON will stumble on, a tired elephant with not much to offer." As most people predicted, the matter has been settled and Alhaji Jimoh Ibrahim, the Harvard trained lawyer that now owns NICON has vowed to make NICON "a model in Africa". We are all waiting to see. With its geographic spread in all parts of the country, it would have been very easy for NICON to make Nigerians embrace life assurance as a religion but NICON only pursues the 'lucrative' NNPC (Nigeria National Petroleum Corporation) account. In a country where less than five percent of the population have life policies, can you see why NICON can never excel?

As I earlier highlighted, insurance companies use independent agents to market their policies and most agents are only interested in the first premium, which is usually theirs for keeps. Immediately the agent signs you on and collects the first premium and turns over your form to the insurance company, he is through with you, and goes out in search for the next victim. From this point you're on your own, at the mercy of the insurance company. Even though that is beginning to change, most insurance companies, especially the old generation companies, still don't have in-house marketing staff of their own. It should have been quite simple at the time for NICON to write to say part of your policy recently matured. Are you happy with our service so far? Do you have any concerns about the policy that you think you should bring to our attention? Should there be any concerns please write to our MR. XYZ of our Customer Service Unit who would be glad to hear from you. That would have given me an opportunity to tell them their service stinks. They would have then been in a position to see what action to take to avoid a repeat occurrence. Actively searching for customers' opinion, encouraging them to complain and creating avenues for such complaints and taking decisive action is the hallmark of the truly great companies. We will look at further ways of soliciting the *voice of the customer* in other Bridges as we continue to explore this interesting subject.

Bridge Seventy Nine

CRAWL ON YOUR KNEES TO THE CUSTOMER YOU HAVE OFFENDED

Crawl on your knees to the customer you have offended is about restitution. Have you done something or has something happened that the customer is unhappy about; and you are convinced the customer was to blame and he should apologize to you and your company for his transgression. Think again! Nobody ever wins a war against the customer. Don't even contemplate it!

Whilst it's not impossible to keep the customer always satisfied, nay delighted, achieving the ultimate is not easy. You must be humble enough to accept this and understand that from time to time you will fall below the customer's expectation in certain respects. The key to excellence is the willingness to try, fail, rise and try again. In short, recovery and marshalling resources to save the situation, learning from the process and improving, is the hallmark of the excellent companies, for excellence is not a destination to be reached, a target to be hit, but a never-ending journey of searching for the best way to serve the customer. Customer service problems should be viewed as opportunities to learn and improve beyond your current mark. And the truth is that the customer is always willing to forgive.

A Mckinsey research earler cited titled *"Why Industrial Companies Lose Customers"*, company indifference was cited as the most important reason for leaving (68%), while other factors such as lower price else where, and relocation, to mention a few, ranked far below at 9% and 3%, respectively. The TARP research earlier quoted indicated that 90% of customers having a bad service experience return if "saved" by a well handled recovery.

Intuit, the Palo Alto based software company in 1992 launched *QuickBooks* software with a critical bug. It took a $1million recovery programme to fix the bug and undo the damage. Within weeks of the fix, *QuickBooks* was a number 1 best seller. In 1991, Mercedes recalled over 1,000 Mercedes 600 C-Class from the North American market to fix the bonnet latch when it was reported that the latch of one of the vehicles failed while on high speed. The cost to Mercedes was $189m but the action restored Mercedes' reputation. Early in 2004 or thereabout, Ford was forced to recall all Ford Navigator SUVs (Sport Utility Vehicles) made the previous six months after a few crashes were linked to faulty tyres supplied by Firestone. The website CRASHWORTHINESS FYI.COM reported that Firestone/Bridgestone eventually recalled 14.4million tyres and are facing an avalanche of lawsuits.

In December 2006 Volkswagen ordered the recall of 300,000 of its Passat models worldwide owing to problems with the windshield wipers, fuel system and breaks. The models affected were produced since 2005. In some, the electrical feed to the windshield wipers broke down when exposed to moisture during heavy rain. In addition, owners of diesel-powered vehicles were asked to inspect them for possible fuel leakage. And in models with 200 horsepower engines, some brakes suffered from defects that compromised their function, though the overall system was not subject to failure. Owners were to be directly contacted by the company about the recall. Volkswagen spokesman declined to estimate how much the recall would cost the company. (Thisday, Tuesday, December 12, 2006).

Contrast the above recall scenarios with Intel's grandstanding in 1994 when it turned out that Intel's prized Pentium chip contained a bug. In a lead feature article in Fortune magazine of December 12, 2005 by Richard S. Tedlow on Intel's co-founder and legendary CEO, Andrew S. Grove, the magazine gave a vivid description of the quagmire Intel found itself. Though Intel's engineers were aware of the problem, they estimated that a spreadsheet user would encounter the problem once every 27,000 years of spreadsheet use so they decided not to report. However the fall after the latest Pentium chip was released, Thomas Nicely, a mathematician at Lynchburg College in Virginia spoted '*inconsistencies*' in the way the chip performed a rare, complex scientific calculation. Nicely's observation was posted on an Internet newsgroup and before long came to public view. Before long IBM announced it would suspend shipments of its Pentium-based computers. All the while Intel's CEO, Andy Grove, kept arguing that the issue was insignificant as though the whole thing was just a technical issue. The more Grove argued the more the uproar grew until Intel was forced to issue an apology to customers and adopt a no-question asked replacement policy. The apology read in part "*What we view as a minor technical problem has taken on a life of its own. We apologize. We were motivated by a belief that replacement is simply unnecessary for most people. We still feel that way.'* Following this apology which some felt Intel was talking down on customers, a customer replied on the internet with a poem:

> *"When in the future we wish to deride*
> *A CEO whose disastrous pride*
> *Causes spokesmen to lie*
> *And sales streams to dry*
> *We'll say he's got Intel Inside* ™"

The Pentium recall cost Intel $475million. You toy with the Bridge *Crawl on Your Knees to the Customer you have offended* at your own peril.

Bridge Eighty

APOLOGIZE TO THE CUSTOMER FOR ALL MISTAKES – CAUSED BY YOU OR NOT

Simple, even trite! You bet. But when did your people last apologize to the customer? Did you forget to return a telephone call, answer an urgent mail, keep the customer waiting for too long at your lobby, anything?

Apologize to the Customer for All Mistakes – Caused by You or Not applies to the big and the small company alike. For the small company especially in the Nigerian environment, the chief risk is illiteracy. You have the business person that has invested his entire live savings in a business and then literally hands over the business to his younger 'brother' to run, while he pursues other more important things like running after contracts in Abuja, Nigeria's federal capital. The 'brother' *manager* has neither education nor training. He doesn't even know why he was asked to man the business in the first place. All he knows is that his brother 'has money.' The big man spends all his time being the 'managing director' and only comes to the business at night to collect the day's sales proceeds.

For the big company the key risk is size, inertia and bureaucracy. Alfred Sloan, the founder of General Motors once lamented GM's mammoth size and concluded that GM's size was an impediment to it ever becoming a leader. When GM was tottering on the brink of bankruptcy Sloan words sounded almost preverbial. Sloan's words "*sometimes I am almost forced to the conclusion that General Motors is so large and its inertia so great that it's impossible for us to be leaders*" may have influenced the new GM's management decision not to pursue size for size's sake any more as a policy but to pursue profitable growth. Seeing what size is doing to Toyota, the decision appears a masterstroke.

The problem of inertia is particularly acute in government establishments where the customer is at best treated as a diversion and at worst as an enemy. Take NIPOST (Nigeria Postal Services). A letter from Ibadan to Lagos (a distance of about 110km) takes 6 weeks to arrive. From Lagos to Kaduna, about 800km, it's also six weeks. Overseas letters are in a special class of their own. A few days ago I received a letter from the UK. It arrived after 30 days, a great improvement over the one I received from India in 1999. It was posted on October 1, 1998 and I received it on April 20, 1999. It had taken the poor letter from the India Institute of Bank Management and Finance 170 days to get to my desk. And during that period, NIPOST had a Post Master General, who every day went went to work at 8.00am and closed at 5pm and collected his salary promptly at the end of every month. Any wonder in Nigeria we say government business is no man's business. Is there a system in place to appraise NIPOST's performance? Who does the appraisal? Is letters turnaround one of the key appraisal parameters? In the US, the Post Master General would have gone to Congress to explain his performance but in Nigeria, such mundane issue as turnaround of letters is of no interest to the National Assembly. What a pity!

NIPOST will blame its woes on Nigeria Railways, which will blame its own woes on Nigeria Coal Mining Company, which will blame it woes on Ministry of Finance, which will blame it on NNPC, and the blame game will continue till thy kingdom come, but nothing will change. Blame and excuses do not solve problems, only actions do. We can lie with our words, but we cannot lie with our actions. Apologizing to the customer means you must keep your ego aside, it means your key managers must keep their egos aside, it means everybody must keep his or her ego aside and be willing to accept that something has gone wrong. What made it to go wrong, how it went wrong, who's to blame do not really matter. What matters is that a prompt apology is tendered to the customer.

Oliver Opara, a lawyer turned banker, related to me the story how he'd commissioned a florist to deliver fresh chrysanthemums to his wife on St. Valentine's Day years back, but after collecting the money the florist did nothing. Apparently the florist was swamped with orders and couldn't care less leaving the brisk business in the shop at Ikoyi to deliver flower at Lekki. Rather than apologize the floral company first claimed they couldn't trace the house, next they claimed they didn't meet anybody in the house. The victim stated that the florist claimed everything under the sun except to apologize. Oliver directed his lawyer to charge the case to court for appropriate restitution. No matter how the case is decided, you can be sure the floral company will be one long standing customer poorer. Many organizations find the idea of tendering apology dangerous because they claim it exposes them to legal claims. Nothing can be farther from the truth. Who ever said apologizing is the same as accepting responsibility? So go out and apologize. Bring all those lost customers back.

Bridge Eighty One

KNOW THAT A COMPLAINING CUSTOMER IS YOUR BEST ALLY

The TARP Research earlier quoted merits a repeat here. Among the key finding of that research was the fact that the great majority of lost cutomers who stopped doing business with a particular organization, 66 per cent left due to poor service, and more tellingly, only about 5 per cent of dissatisfied customers complain. Another way of looking at the fact that only 5 per cent of dissatisfied customers complain is that a whopping 95 per cent of customers having a bad service experience will not complain to you directly. They just simply walk away. It therefore makes sense to actively *encourage* your customers to complain about your service. They should also praise your people when they excel, but here we are concerned only with complaints. Excellent organizations go to great lengths to get feedback from their customers. Some of the methods employed to solicit feedback include providing toll free numbers, giving out simple questionnaires to customers to complete after each service encounter, giving out tokens (which can be redeemed) to customers to encourage them to complain.

Sewell's Village Cadillac Company Inc., one of the most consistently profitable automobile dealerships in Dallas, Forth Worth, and San Antonio we earlier mentioned gives out a three-sentence questionnaire to customers that ask the customer whether they are completely satisfied. Their website www.sewell.com is replete with countless testimonials from satisfied customers from across the US. Carl Sewell's book (written with Paul Brown), **Customers for Life**, is a must read on the issue of measurements.

It's necessary that you actively encourage customers to complain otherwise they will not complain to you directly, as research has shown. The reasons most customers don't like to complain, amongst others, include:

(a) they have no confidence their complaints will make a difference
(b) they may be regarded as cantankerous and a nuisance
(c) they may be barred from the company.

It is for this reason that you should actively encourage the customer to complain. For example, you can post toll free numbers as we mentioned earlier where the customer can call to log complaints, and the name of the specific individuals they should call should be given. Whenever there is a complaint, write to the customer and acknowledge the complaint; inform the customer what you are going to do about his complaint, and when you are going to do it, and finally, invite the customer to try you again.

There is nothing more reassuring to the customer that a responsible person is taking active interest in his complaints. On the other hand the customer feels betrayed when his complaints are ignored. Sometimes the customer has to write to the CEO before something is done about his complaints. This usually happens in organizations where quality is 'everyone's' job and therefore no man's job. While quality is really everyone's job, measurement of quality must be assigned to a specific unit. Handling of complaints is part of the measurement process.

PART 7

The Icing on the Service Excellence Cake

Bridge Eighty Two

HAVE A HOTLINE FOR CUSTOMERS WHO NEED HELP FAST

A hotline is for emergencies. It is a dedicated line preserved exclusively for special traffic. During the cold war, when the then two superpowers pursued MAD (Mutually Assured Destruction) policies, there was a hotline between the Kremlin and the White House. With the hotline they could inform each other they would never be mad enough to push the button first.

Have you ever faced a life threatening emergency and you wished 'something' could happen, a miracle, to reverse the situation. In 1988 I faced that kind of emergency situation. Winnie, then 3, and Socrates, then 1, my kids, contracted diarrhea and were vomiting seriously. I was away at work. I came back to meet them totally dehydrated. The ORT (oral rehydration therapy) prescription administered by Aret, my wife, seemed not to have any effect. I was desperate. The thing I needed most at that moment was a *hotline* to the local hospital. There was none. Now, you can imagine the sense of anger, frustration and helplessness that I felt.

Sometimes the situation is not life threatening. The customer may just require information from you. Now, you may ask, why can't the customer use the general line? The thing is the general line is not meant for emergencies. The general line is meant for day - to - day business calls. The hotline on the other hand is a dedicated line manned by people who have been trained and have information at their finger tips and can answer questions posed by customers. Most often than not, organizations don't have what some forward looking companies have come to call *Solutions Lines* and customers have no where to turn to for vital information about products and services. When next you think what to do to make helping the customer with information an integral arsenal in your service armoury, think *Solutions Line* with capital 'S' and 'L'. Among the banks, Diamond Bank recently implemented a toll free number 0808CALLDBC. Happily, other banks are following suit and the banking system is the better for it.

Bridge Eighty Three

KNOW ALL YOUR CUSTOMERS BY NAME

You're in a crowded square in an unfamiliar city where people are playing a strange game. You try to figure out what it is they're into. You're lost in your thoughts when suddenly one of the players shouts your name. She is totally ecstatic and makes you feel welcome. You're not sure you know her but her enthusiasm is infectious. She explains how the game is played - the rules, the players, what you need to do to win in this game and what you need to do to avoid losing. For the time you're there, you are the cynosure of all eyes. Before long you have joined in playing the game. You know the name of all the other players and now you're on a first name basis. You feel tall, you feel happy, and you feel you belong. You're no more a stranger.

Now flip the coin over. You're in this strange place where nobody knows you. You see one or two guys who you think you know but when you try to introduce yourself you're rebuffed. You see another guy that you think you know and you smile and start by saying I'm... but before you can finish the sentence the guy informs you that he doesn't know you and walks away. Now you're really uncomfortable. What is left of your self confidence is shattered.

Strangely, all but few organizations treat their customers in the later manner. You have staff who will deal with the customer year in and year out and yet will not take the time to do something as basic as knowing the name of the person he is dealing with. In this regard, banks are the worst offenders, especially the old generation banks where the colored plastic tally was once in vogue. To address the customer they call the number written on the tally and the colour the plastic is made of. So you become number 20 blue or number 10 black. Nothing was more demeaning. Though the practice is no more in vogue in the cities, the tally still hold sway outside big cities.

You must know that when a customer is in your premises, he is out of his comfort zone. No matter how long the customer has been doing business with you don't expect him to be completely at ease in your own environment. In the first place you have your own small world that is understood only by people in your organization. This ranges from the way you address one another, the way you talk, the way you greet one another, the unspoken communication, and a whole series of things. Together this is sometimes called the corporate culture. Only you and your colleagues can become members of this special world. If any outsider, including your customer, tries to penetrate this special world of yours, he will be met by an invisible barrier.

You and you alone as a service provider can break down this barrier. One of the best ways to do this is to address the customer by his name. It goes without saying that you cannot address the customer by his name unless you know his name. Whether you address your customer by his first name or the middle or the last name is for the customer to decide. Just ask the customer and ask with genuine interest. Sometimes the customer may prefer as a mark of courtesy that you add mister to his name, especially those customers who are older than you in age. So address the customer as Paul or Mr. Uduk or Mr. Cyril. Again some customers will rather you addressed them as 'sir'. Fine and good go ahead. But don't forget, the sweetest word in the world any man likes to hear is his name, not number 5 red!

Bridge Eighty Four

KNOW ALL YOUR CUSTOMERS' FRIENDS

You have just had a warm bath after a hectic day in the office and you are now well relaxed, able to hear people out. Your wife tells you that she was in the post office earlier in the day and she met a certain man who greeted her warmly and introduced himself as working in the plumbing company that did an excellent plumbing job in your house the previous weekend. He was not in the team that did the actual job but he is the supervisor of that team and the team leader had briefed him about the family. She informs you that the man actually assisted her meander out of chaotic traffic and had extended his greetings to you.

You blink your eyes and recall that the man's name is Sunday and is the supervisor in the plumbing company in the next street. Even though you personally know Sunday, you didn't know Sunday knows your wife. You're understandably proud of Sunday and you quite appreciate his kind gesture towards your wife. On balance when you have another plumbing job, you are going to remember Sunday's company. That's the power of the Bridge *Know All Your Customer's Friends*.

What your wife told you is a testimonial about Sunday and in delivering service, nothing works more wonders than good testimonials. Knowing all your customer's friends and being nice to them, going all out to also assist them in the little ways that you can greatly increase your leverage for good testimonials. Your customer's friends include every body connected to your customer. This includes the spouse, if your customer is married, the kids, co-workers, associates and a host of other connected people. Do not underestimate the power of testimonials, especially, the word of mouth type!

Birds of the same feather as they saying goes flock together. Right! So if your customer is good enough for you, his friends most probably should be good enough for you. It makes sense. So how many of your customer's friends do you know, male and female.

Let's assume you're a marketing officer in a bank. Who are your best 20 customers? Who are your best customers' best 20 male friends? Who are your best customers' best 20 female friends? 20+20+20 = 60. If by this simple or silly idea you can increase the number of your customers by 300 per cent, doesn't it make sense that you know all your customer's friends? As we have observed time and time again in this book, everything boils down to perception. Let your customer sell you to his friends. Don't forget words of mouth carry more credibility. Get down to business. Get all the details about your customer's friends. And who is the best person to let you into this secret than your customer. Let him tell you their birth day, their wife's birthday, their children birthday, their club and professional society, what they value most, their hobbies and you are on your way to building enduring relationship with your customer's friends. As a matter of fact, there are business intelligence software packages from SAS (see www.sas.com) that are quite affordable that the small business can acquire to run its business intelligently. In today's flat world, you simply can't afford to run your business as in the days of Lord Lugard.

Bridge Eighty Five

KNOW EVERYTHING YOUR CUSTOMER LIKES

If your customer belongs to one of the fringe religions, should you become interested in that? The simple answer is yes. If your customer is a jockey enthusiast, become a jockey enthusiast.

To know everything your customer likes, you must keep learning by the day. Your knowledge must be built up over a period of years or even decades. In Bridge One we said *Know Your Customer*. That probably makes Bridge Eighty Five redundant. Well not quite. While the Bridge *Know Your Customer* is concerned more with modelling the service to the specific target market segment you wish to serve, *Know Everything Your Customer Likes* drills it down to a more granular level, to the level of the individual customer. Let's illustrate with a fine example from Robert Spector and Patrick D. McCarthy's **The Nordstrom Way,** the book that went behind the scenes to tell us how Nordstrom has managed to stay on top of the pack in customer service decades after decades. The story centred on Patrice Nagasawa, a customer service representative who worked in the Bellevue Square Savvy department. Although she worked in the apparel department of the super store, Patrice incredibly considered herself to be in the '*time saving business,*' as most of her best customers hardly set foot in the store! These customers preferred to order mechandise by phone and Patrice simply mailed to them. On top of that Patrice also had many "*drive-by*" customers. They call Patrice in the morning to inform her what they are looking for, then they call her when they are getting close to the store and call again when they are right outside the store and Patrice dashes out to show them what she has chosen for them. They indicate what they want and she dashes back to the store, rings up the purchases and brings them to the customer's car and they drive away without ever setting foot in the store. Patrice said "*I've developed that trust with these customers because they know I'm not going to abuse it.*"

As you can see, Patrice Nagasawa's style is the essence of the Bridge *Know Everything Your Customer Likes.* Innovation and creativity are the names of the game here as with all other Bridges. Markets have so fragmented that *one-size-fits-all* type of service will just not do in today's world where what was just a cool product an hour ago is reduced to a mere commodity the next hour, as the Apple iPod has gradually found itself. You have to keep thinking constantly. You have to constantly scan the environment and interpret what you observe accordingly and quickly implement strategies to ensure the customer is never left in the lurch.

Another example from **Why Satisfied Customers Defect** by Thomas O. Jones and W. Earl Sasser, Jr. further illustrates the point of this Bridge. This story was about a movie theater. Anybody that has been to Silverbird Galaria in Victoria Island, Lagos, by mid-morning on a Saturday will understand the frustration of getting a parking space there. Sometimes even if you have found a place to park, you may be frustrated when trying to leave as another guest may have parked behind you. Jones and Sasser's story was about such a movie facility somewhere in the Southwest of the US. To reduce frustration about parking and queuing to buy ticket and improve the customer's general movie-going experience, the theater managers posted attendants two blocks away from the theater to sell tickets and facilitate car parking. On top of that, the theater started serving food throughout the facility so guests didn't have to leave the viewing area in search of what to eat. Even seated customers began to be served until the movie began. As an icing on the movie cake, bathrooms began to be cleaned four times per hour. As the authors put it, *"The end result: a large number of highly satisfied, highly loyal customers."*

Knowing everything that your customer likes sometimes may involve a heavy dose of unlearning what you already know both at the individual and at the corporate levels. While today's mantra is constant learning, which has spawned ideas such as Compulsory Continuous Professional Development (CCPD), Mandatory Lifelong Learning (MLL) and the like, it's amazing how many organisations fail to discern that the flip side of continuous learning is continuous unlearning. Don't forget, at first the earth was thought to be flat; the best and most prescient scientists and philosophers of middle ages believed and even *proved* mathematically that the sun revolved round the earth. The Holy Roman Empire even endorsed and passed edicts to uphold these 'self-evident truths.' However, these edicts did not stop people like Copernicus from thinking hard, querying and laying down his life to disprove the self-evident truths.

For daring to theorise that the earth rotated round the sun, in support of Copernicus, Gallileo was sentenced to death, that was later communted to house arrest for life. Despite the threat to his life, Gallileo refused to recant. At the turn of the nineteenth century, people queried the feasibility of Carl Benz's and Henry Ford's contraptions, later to be called motorcar, *that would travel faster than a horse-drawn cart at 15 kilometers per hour*. Now we know better. When Ford decided to double his workers' pay in 1914, other industrialists derided the move by saying "the most foolish thing ever attempted." New York Times, ever the conservative, proclaimed, "he's crazy, isn't he?", and Wall Street Journal rationalised, "the application of spiritual principles where they don't belong."

Why wasn't General Motors the first to come up with the idea of fuel efficient cars, even in the face of Arab oil embargo, but Toyota? Why wasn't IBM that invented the personal computer but two unknown guys, with Steve as their first names, fooling around in a garage and having fun? Why wasn't the Swiss watch empire that commercialized the *quartz* technology but amateurs *unschooled* in watch movement technology in far away Japan? Beware your so-called professional standard may be no less than one man's myopic view of how the world should be and has no relevance to the way the customer *thinks* much less what he wants.

As I earlier highlighted, I'm a subscriber to Starcomms internet service. Starcomms has three bouquets of service: 24 hours, 12 hours (9am to 9pm) and 12 hours (9pm to 9am). Initially while still in paid employment I subscribed to the 9am to 9pm service and only used Starcomms's internet service on weekends, for a total of less than 15 hours out of the 50 hours I'm entitled to per month, since Starcomms has no flexi-plan, whereby you pay as you surf in the comfort of your home. To get that service required my going to a business center, which sometimes was not very comfortable. Now I subscribe for the 24 hour service for a maximum of 100 hours or 30 days which ever comes first. If the service expires at 12 midnight I'm shut out automatically because Starcomms does not know me individually as a person even though I have been using their service for some five years now. Because of this Starcomms misses the opportunity to tailor its services to my exact needs. Starcomms may give you a thousand and one reasons why flexi-service cannot work in Nigeria. It may quote demographic studies by the National Census Board, or GDP figures from the World Bank but don't be deceived. The moment someone arrives the scene with internet flexi-service, NITEL's fate may befall Starcomms. Look at the fierce competion that is now taking place in the satellite broadcasting industry. Before Multichoice had total monopoly and their services was targetted at the elites. However, since HITV and Startimes arrived the scene, subscription rates have fallen sharply, with Multichoice showing flexibility in line with the changing market space. Even at the risk of sounding unduly repetitive, companies and all organisations for that matter that refuse to see things from the outside in, that is, from the customer's perspective, and innovate accordingly, be they banks, hotels, airlines, telecos, schools, hospitals, restaurants, fast foods, churches, government departments and agencies, will find themselves increasingly irrelevant.

Bridge Eighty Six

SHARE YOUR CUSTOMER'S HAPPY MOMENTS

Share your customer's happy moments goes beyond the traditional public relations. Public relation as we know is usually a one-off affair. In sharing our customer's happy moments, we are looking at a planned programme of structured and sustained relationship building measures that keep us closely connected to the customer. This ensures that you're always a part of the customer's close ring of *friends*.

The idea of sharing the customer's happy moments is gradually catching on, especially with banks. Nowadays, bank marketing officers attend their customer's and their children's birthday parties, they attend their *naming, house warming* and wedding ceremonies, they participate in celebrating the arrival of the new born, burial of close relatives and loved ones. Towards the end of last year, I was mildly surprised to see the photograph of one of the ED's of a top Nigerian bank dressed as an Hindu, with chalk marks on the face to boot. He'd gone to India, I learnt, to a attend the wedding ceremony of the son of one of the bank's top customers!

At the corporate level, companies congratulate their customers during major milestones in the customer's history and when their customers make major technological breakthroughs. Sharing your customer's happy moments is all part of the game. Don't miss such opportunities.

Bridge Eighty Seven

STAND BY THE CUSTOMER
WHEN ALL IS NOT WELL

Donald Trump, the real estate mogul, with his flamboyant lifestyle and a knack for eccentricity was probably the most well known American bankrupt of the 80s. The spectacular collapse of his vast business empire was the most reported event in America in 1988 through 1990. The O. J. Simpson murder trial and the Clinton impeachment trial combined did not equal the headlines Trump captured. Trump lost all his friends, including all his banker friends and financiers. Describing the bankrupt Trump, Wayne Barrett, in his book, *Trump: The Deals and the Downfall*, quoted New York developer Sam Lefak as saying of Trump, *"today he's a peacock, and tomorrow he's a feather duster"*. How wrong Sam Lefak was!

Trump, never the pessimist, had predicted he would be the *"greatest comeback of the century."* By 1998, ten years after the fall, Trump was right back at the top. Today most of the finest hotels in New York bear his name, TRUMP, with capital T.

Bankers are the worst fair weather friends. Of this we quote George Bernard Shaw once again: *"a banker is someone who gives you his umbrella when the sun is shining and wants it back the moment it starts to rain."* Truly failure is an orphan. No one likes to associate with a failure but in a one-to-one business relationship, this should not be the case. It's when things are really down that the customer needs you the more, especially if the customer has not commited any fraud but simply suffered business downturn. It is at such times that the customer needs alternative insights to what the problem could be, this is the time to counsel, this is the time to analyze the situation together, this is the time to provide additional support. If you stand by your customer when all is not well, he will surely reward you when the situation turns around. As the Americans say, what goes around turns around. But don't be penny wise and pound foolish, sometimes it may just be the right thing to advise your customer to cut his loses and move on.

Bridge Eighty Eight

HAVE CLEAN DRINKING WATER AVAILABLE – THE CUSTOMER MAY REQUEST FOR A GLASS

Straight forward, isn't it? Think about it! I had the experience of eating at NANET, the fast food and restaurant chain based in Kaduna and requesting for drinking water. You know what the waiter told me? This is what, *"we don't give people water, you have to buy Coke"*. I told the young lady I didn't want to drink Coca Cola. Well, the young lady brought our discussion to an end when she told me that that was the policy but she could assist me buy SWAN (bottled) water if I wanted to.

I found this policy quite strange because in the whole of Nigeria, it's customary to offer food along with water. You can't separate the two. Why should restaurants be different? I brought the matter up with Ini Akpabio, the CEO of NANET, who happened to be known to me. I pointed out the cultural link between food and water in Africa and the need to provide service taking into consideration our cultural milieu. I advised Ini to adopt everything good in the African culture and make the service as natural as possible. I advised Ini to give customers the option of having either the company's freshly boiled water or bottled water. Ini thanked me and promised to drop the 'no water except Coke' policy immediately. That was in 1993. NANET implemented the policy because the next time I went there I was served freshly boiled water.

It does not really matter the nature of your business. Africa is such a hot oven. You have the customer coming in from the street sweating all over and he asks please can I have some water to drink? And you look at him again wondering if the man knows what he is talking about? You just go and find the man water to drink. As the scout motto goes, *Always Prepared!* It's such little things that will endear you to the customer. The business is not a charity organization but by giving him that water and making him comfortable he will buy more from you and will tell his friends about how kind you are. Sometimes the customer may not settle for your freshly boiled water as the source may be suspect. That is why most companies now have water dispensers, complete with disposable cups, for customers and staff alike. For a large corporate organization, of course, this is the right thing. The mom-and pop shop should not forget there is always the freshly boiled water option - which should of course come with a guarantee and sparkling glasses.

As with all other Bridges in this book, the Bridge *Have Clean Drinking Water Available, The Customer May Ask For A Glass* can be uncannily deceptive. Here we use water and clean drinking glasses to illustrate the point, but beware, cleanliness applies to all other areas. Take the case of the toilet, which the Americans call bathroom. In 99 per cent of organizations I've visited in Nigeria, this area is always an eyesore. Since senior executives have their own personal toilets, no one really cares much about the general toilet used by the other staff. Most organizations do not allow 'outsiders', call that customers, access to their staff toilets and where they do, it's the dirtiest toilet that 'outsiders' are allowed to use. This again is where Diamond Bank excels. The bank out-sources the cleaning of its offices in the Lagos area to the Lekki-based cleaning company, Teknokleen. Teknokleen goes to great lengths, cleaning the water closets every 15 minutes, to ensure the toilets are clean and always freshly scented. You can actually sit down and eat in some of the toilets if you care. They are always spick and span. Other banks, especially the first generation banks need to take a cue from Diamond Bank in this regard. Without mentioning names, most of the toilets in these banks that I have discreetly inspected and actually used left sour taste in my mouth. Most fast foods are equally quilty of stinking water closets, with the worst offender being the old generation chain with branches all over the country.

Talking about clean drinking water, MONA and Slakers seem to have taken the lead in supplying water in 25 litre plastic kegs to companies for use in their water dispensers. I suspect, together, they control some 60% of the market. But what do MONA and Slakers do? They supply dirty plastic kegs, which most companies unbeliveably accept without question and use in their corporate water dispensers! When you go to work tomorrow, cross check especially if you work in a bank. I noticed the dirty, totally unpresentable plastic kegs in bank hallways and started taking pictures and I have a stack of them now. Request, in fact, demand the company that supplies plastic kegs for use in your company's water dispensers to meticulously wash the kegs before passing your gate. Detail your security operatives to carry out the checking.

Bridge Eighty Nine

ALLOW THE CUSTOMER ACCESS TO YOUR PHONE, FAX, WATER CLOSET AND ALL

The telephone is the easiest and fastest means to keep in touch with the rest of the world. The customer may need to make a call while in your office. Now everybody has cellular phone so the point might not be that important but be on the alert just in case. Allow the customer to use your phone, fax, computer, photocopying machine, printer, water closet and all if asked. You may think this gesture would cost you money, but on the contrary, it will bring you more money. Why? The simple reason is that the customer will be happy with you.

Allowing the customer to make phone call, to fax or photocopy in your office send important message to the customer that you care, that you value him. In fact, the closer or tighter your relationship is with the customer, the better. It is this sort of relationship that is spurning corporate alliances at the multinational level. All you have to know is that everything starts small, then you discover synergy in your different cooperative endeavors, then you start sharing strategic information, integrating systems and so on. Welcome the customer to work in your premises if he needs to. Some companies will not allow customers access to their water closet! Sometimes the clean water closet is reserved for the manager while the customer may be allowed access to the junior staff's, usually damaged toilet, dripping water. How demeaning can you get!

Bridge Ninety

KEEP YOUR MESSAGE SHORT AND SWEET WHEN COMMUNICATING WITH THE CUSTOMER

I found this message on the door of a small company in Aries Block, Elaganza Plaza, Apapa:

NOTICE!

NO VISITOR IS ALLOWED IN THIS OFFICE EXCEPT ON OFFICIAL APPOINTMENT!
ENDEARVOUR TO BE VERY BRIEF WHILE YOU ARE ALLOWED IN!!
ALWAYS SCRUB THE UNDERNEATH OF YOUR SHOES/SLIPPERS ON THE FOOT-MAT BEFORE ENTRY!!!
KINDLY COMPLY WITH THESE INSTRUCTIONS TO AVOID EMBARRASSMENT!!!!

SIGNED: MANAGEMENT

The above message is short, but ask yourself, is this message sweet? All your message should be kept short and sweet. Don't offend your audience in your mails. Don't write to impress but to express. It's customary in Nigeria to conclude corporate memos, especially those that emanate from HR (now HCM) departments, to the effect that the action should be carried out "with immediate effect." As if that was not enough, just the other day I read a memo addressed to "all staff" of Dangote Flour. It was issued by "Chief Security" and was pasted right by the entrance door to their main office on the third floor of Marble House, Falomo, Ikoyi. It expressed 'shock' and 'concern' over staff non-challant attitude to their ID cards. It informed staff that anyone caught breaking 'the law' of wearing or not wearing ID cards will be 'seriously dealt with'. 'The law', the memo went on, applied while staff were on or off duty. If you investigate the background of 'Mr. Chief Security' he is likely to be an ex-soldier or ex-police officer. Most people attribute the militaristic tone of memos in Nigeria to the military psyche passed down after 33 years (1966 -1999) of military rule in Nigeria. Note however madam HCM personnel and chief security officer that you're not in the military barracks and your audience do not wear military uniforms. If you think the expressions ''with immediate effect'', ''the law'', and ''dealt with'' make you sound important, well I can just tell you that they make you pass off as an uncouth brat with no sense of decency.

Bridge Ninety One

DON'T ASK FOR FAVOURS FROM THE CUSTOMER

Asking for favors from customers in a developing country like Nigeria where workers are paid a pittance for wages is all too common. This is especially so in the so called *'one man companies'*, not-for-profit organizations, and even giant banks where the use of *'associate staff'* is the norm. Underlying the problem of actively harassing customers for favours, especially cash inducements, as you might have guessed is poverty. Poverty literally walks naked in the streets. Whether it's a bank, restaurant, bookshop, insurance agency, stock broking, law or accounting firm, the process is always invariably the same. The moment you enter the shop, say, the sales girl, okay let's say lady, smiles at you, and you ask 'how's the day'?, and She answers 'tank God' (for thank God). Moments later she tells you either by body language or directly that she's not been paid for three months and that she's hungry. Sometimes she might tell you 'do us (referring to herself) *Christmas, Easter, Sallah, happy new month, happy New Year*, depending on the time of the year. You might think she's kidding but she's dead serious. She might be well dressed, with a dazzling coiffure, but that's immaterial.

This book, however, is for serious minded companies that know that the stakes are too high and will not pay their people peanuts. As the saying goes, if you pay your people peanuts, expect to get monkeys. Make it a part of your culture that asking for favors from the customer is unacceptable. Some times workers ask for favours without uttering a word. Watch the eyes, watch the total body language. Sometimes the message is hi, we've done all this and provided you with such *helluva* service and you have not even noticed us. Bank Tellers, Note Counters, Cashiers in super markets are the most adept at this. Be careful customers may come to believe it's part of the price they have to pay in order to get good service if each time they come your body language suggests, hey, have you noticed my great service and won't you do something for me! Provide good service as naturally as you breathe in and breathe out and let your reward come from the good market rating of your company, the good pay therefrom and the complete personal satisfaction that comes from serving humanity.

Bridge Ninety Two

Don't Talk Down On The Customer

Is the customer really "The King" or "The Queen"? While the customer may not necessarily wear a crown like Her Majesty, judge by yourself whether indeed 'The King' should be addressed the way this directive from one of the top banks addressed one of their customers on March 31, 2011. "Effective April 1, 2011, the monthly charge on DBXA Starter account would change from N1,500 to N1,750. Other features remain the same. For details call 012793500." The message was not signed. It is short, but ask yourself, is it sweet? Every time you are tempted to send a condescending mail to your customer, remember he is 'The King' and should be addressed with deference, respect and courtesy. The customer may not always have a say in what you do, but be rest assured, he will at the end of the day have his way.

Epilogue

THINK UP ONE MILLION NEW BRIDGES TO THE CUSTOMER'S HEART, NOW!

Quality has come a full cycle, from the purely mechanistic notion of *quality of products*, to the second dimension encapsulated in *quality of service,* to the third dimension of *customer care,* and to the fourth dimension embedded in *customer experience.* Some organisations believe with technology, they can jump to the ultimate customer experience by installing expensive PABX systems to answer telephone calls, so when you call them instead of talking with a human being, you speak with a machine, which tells you, ''all lines are busy, you're number fifty on the queue.'' Yet when you visit these same companies no one you meet in the lobby greets you as everybody is rushing for a meeting. You visit their water closets you see things your eyes cannot take. We engage in lies and self denial that we can serve the customer without internalising the basics: simple courtesy and warmth. We overate ambience and forget fire and passion. We think about design in terms of how it looks forgetting it's all about how it works. We pay lip service to customer and staff retention and focus on sending our managers to the best business schools, preferably Harvard and Wharton. Lies, lies and damned lies.

All the lies in the world will not make you great. Only enthusiastic customers and dynamically engaged employees will make you great. Customers and employees are the two sides of the same coin. They are variously referred to as external and internal customers. Great organizations go to great lengths to win their hearts, minds and souls. Mediocre organizations pay lip service to customer and employee retention and engagement. Mediocre organizations retain the best parking slots in their premises for their top brass. At their car parks you'll see 'cars parked at owner's risk' boldly displayed. Great organizations instinctively know that the little things matter. Like reserving convenient parking for customers, and like promoting their people when due. They know that the only thing that matters is the law of action. Action wins, not the words we say because we can lie with our words but we cannot lie with our actions.

All the lies in the world will not make you great. A wise man once said, the fact that someone is willing to lay down his life for an idea does not necessarily make the idea correct. If you wish to know how great you are, just go and ask your customers and employees. Only the market place determines who is great and who is mediocre. The market place rewards great companies. The society at large respects great companies and their leaders. To the customer, the size of your balance sheet, the type of car your CEO drives, the décor of your CFO's office mean nothing. Whether the floor of your reception area is made of marble or granite is certainly immaterial to the customer, all he wants to know is what you have in stock for him, and how you make him feel. To the employee, the only thing that matters is that all your actions tell him he is valued. Letting your people have the first crack at the latest opening in the organization says more than all the tonnes of verbiage you put in between the covers of your glossy annual report. Size will not safe you. The popular press despite awarding you with all forms of awards will desert you when the time comes. That you are as old as Methusella and have had a glorious past is irrelevant to the market place, ask Union Bank of Nigeria Plc., the once elegant stallion.

There is more bad news and there is good news. First, the bad news! Stellar good service may not necessarily guarantee your survival. Within a short span of 10 years (1982 – 1992), more than half the class of 'excellent companies' statistically documented in *In Search of Excellence* had gone from excellent to also ran or disappeared altogether. Wang Computers, Apple, IBM, you name it. Under Lou Gerstner, IBM, the once American icon, staged a spectacular come back, but you can be rest assured that things will never be the same again for Big Blue. And for Apple, the story is the same. Try as mercurial Steve Jobs may, you can be rest assured Apple is today a far cry from its halcyon days. Its market share has declined to about 5 per cent overall despite innovative 'cool' products with respectable market shares such as the Apple iPod, iPhone, iTunes and the rest. Gone are the beer busts, pirates' skull and bones. And it's the same Apple that reduced computers from container size machines understood only by computer geeks and engineers to desk top toys accessible to all.

Now, the good news! Quality may not safe you, but without it you will surely die. Think of 3M, Citigroup, Nokia, Siemens. With more than two hundred years history behind each of these companies they remain in the league of the world's most admired companies, thanks in no small measure to their focus on the customer. Their focus on the customer has helped them to not only survive but thrive. Their focus on the customer has enabled them go through the years to see the changes in their industry and market space and even though they stumble from time to time, they have the resilience to rise and reinvent themselves.

Believe it or not, there are no limits to what you can do to satisfy, delight or WOW! the customer. Only remember, everything is focused on the customer. It's all common sense. Take an organization with say 100,000 internal customers and assume everyone in the organization is a center of excellence. What do you get? You get 100,000 centers of excellence. Let loose the creative imagination of these people, get bureaucracy off their back and the people can do wonders.

In his *Iacocca, An Autobiography*, Lee Iacocca, writing with William Novak, relates that while Ford and the other Detroit auto makers were coming out with one new car design every five years, Toyota was coming out with a new model every six months and if I may add, every new model had something new to offer the customer. That was more than 20 years ago! Today Toyota and Honda bring out new models every week. In fact with Toyota and Honda, you can have a car made exactly to your taste and shipped to your garage within two weeks if you're willing to pay for it. It was Jan Carlzon then of Scandinavian Airlines Systems that said *"we are not seeking to be 1,000 per cent better at any one thing, but 1 per cent better at 1,000 things."* The challenge is clear, think of one million new ways to the customer's heart!

Just as Toyota, Honda, ABB, Ritz Carlton, Nordstrom, Marriot, South West Airlines, Nokia, Samsung, LG, Zenith, Nestle and hundreds of other unsung organizations can do it, your company too can do it. What does it take? Literally nothing, just your collective will, imagination and ability to dare. There are structured ways to gather ideas that are literally gathering cobwebs in your people's minds. Focus groups, brainstorming, mind storming, suggestion box, day dreaming, synectics, you name it, can be used to gather ideas that you can use as bridges to the customer's heart. As Fred Crawley, the then Chairman, Alliance and Leicester Building Society, and Chairman, Girobank, stated in the paper he delivered at the 21st Cambridge Seminar of The Chartered Institute of Bankers (as it was then called) held at Christ's College, Cambridge, in September 1993, entitled **Total Quality Management: A Customer Focused Strategy for Business Improvement**, admonished in the concluding part of that paper, "*.... if once quality was a winning ticket, it is now no more than an admission ticket.*" Fred Crawley warned companies that fall short on quality that they will go out of business. He drew participants' attention to the fact that Japanese companies were already seizing the high ground in the service battle by applying to service quality "*the same intensity, passion and detailed implementation that they brought to product quality.*" In reflecting on the urgency of the situation Fred Crawley wondered if the high hopes for reward that the UK financial services industry had for quality was already doomed from the start given the Japanese's commanding lead and concluded that the price of not pursuing quality with even greater fervor would be even higher. He then challenged participants to redouble their resolve and take the quality war to its logical conclusion. In bracing for the trip, Fred Crawley reminded the participants that the journey for quality was for the brave hearted, and as a war commander in the mold of General Eisenhower would in arousing the enthusiasm of his troops, he concluded, "*It is now inevitable as well as urgent and it will not be easy.*"

JOIN *BRIDGES TO THE CUSTOMER'S HEART* FAN CLUB

Has someone touched your heart with a service that was out of this world? Share your heart with the rest of humanity. Visit the website below and let us hear your story, especially heroics, highlighting what, how, where, when it happened and how that changed your relationship with the service provider. We will make sure your story is published in subsequent editions of this book with full credit to you. You can equally develop new Bridges to the Customer's Heart, which will be used in future editions. What a company can do to uplift the customer's heart is endless but here are samplers:

❖ Help the Stranded Customer

❖ Don't Tell the Customer What You Can't Repeat In The Presence Of Your Chairman

❖ Don't Keep The Customer In The Dark About Changes In Your Company

❖ Speak No Evil About The Competition - Let Your Service Do It!

❖ Shut Up If You Have Nothing to Offer the Customer

❖ Pay for the Customer Who Falls Sick On Your Premises

❖ Do To the Customer Everything Your Coy Would Be Proud To Hear

❖ Do Not Complain and Grumble In The Presence of The Customer

❖ Under Promise, Over Deliver

❖ Constantly Re-sharpen Your Service Edge

Website: www.bridgestothecustomersheart.com

Reference

Al Ries & Jack Trout, *The 22 Immutable Laws of Marketing, Violet Them at Your Own Risk,* Harper Business, 1994

Alvin Toffler, *Future Shock*, Random House, 1970

Ayodeji B. Badiru and Babatunde J. Ayeni, *Practitioner's Guide to Quality and Process Improvement*, Chapman & Hall, London, 1993.

Carl Sewell and Paul B. Brown, *The Golden Rules of Customer Care*, Century Business, London, 1992

Carmine Gallo, The Presentation Secrets of Steve Jobs: How to Be Insanely Great in Front of Any Audience, McGraw-Hill, 2010

David T. Kearns and David A. Nadler, *Prophets in the Dark: How Xerox Reinvented Itself and Beat Back the Japanese,* HarperBusiness, 1992

Faith Popcorn, *The Popcorn Report: Faith Popcorn on The Future of Your Company, Your World, Your Life*, Harper Business, New York, 1992

Fredrick F. Reichheld, *The Loyalty Effect, The Hidden Force Behind Growth, Profits, and Lasting Value,* Harvard Business School Press, Boston Massachusetts, 1996

Fortune, The Education of Andy Grove, Richard S. Tedlow, Dec. 12, 2005, page 32

Fortune, The Tragedy of General Motors, Carol J. Loomis, February 27, 2006, page 31

Fortune, How Toyota Does It, Alex Taylor III, March 13, 2006, page 61

Fortune, Samsung Moves Up the Ranks, Stephanie N. Mehta, September 10, 2007, page 12.

Huge E. C. (Ed.) *Total Quality: The Manager's Guide for the 1990s,* Kogan Page, London, 1992

Jack Welch, with Suzy Welch, *Winning,* Harper Business, 2005

Joe Girard (with Stanley H. Brown), *How to Sell Anything to Anybody,* Warner Books, 1977

J. R. Vertin (ed), *Managing the Investment Firm*, AIMR/The Institute of Chartered Financial Analysts, New York, March 1993

John Naisbitt and Patricia Aburdene, *Megatrends 2000: Ten New Directions for The 1990s,* William Morrow & Company, 1990

John Nathan, *Sony The Private Life*, Harper Collins Business, 1999

Ken Blanchard and Mark Miller, *The Secret: What Great Leaders Know and Do*, Berrett-Koehler Publishers, Inc., San Francisco, 2004

Kenichi Ohmae, *The Mind of the Strategist: The Art of Japanese Business,* McGrawHill, 1982

Kevin L. Freiberg and Jacquelyn L. Frieberg, *NUTS! Southwest Airlines Crazy Recipe for Business & Personal Success*, Texere Publishing, London, 2001

Laura A. Liswood, *Serving Them Right*, Harper Business, New York, 1991

Laurie Beth Jones, *Jesus CEO, Using Ancient Wisdom for Visionary Leadership*, Hyperion, 1995

Lee Iacocca, (with William Novak), *Iacocca, An Autobiography*, Bantam Books, 1984

Louis V. Gerstner, Jr., *Who Says Elephants Can't Dance?: Inside IBM's Historic Turnaround*, Harper Business, New York, 2002

Mark Sanborn, *The Fred Factor: How Passion in Your Work and Life Can Turn the Ordinary into the Extraordinary*, WaterBrook Press, 2004

Peter Ellwood, *Implementing Total Quality at TSB* in the book: *Financial Services*: *The Search for Quality*, Seminar Proceedings, The Chartered Institute of Bankers, London, 1993

Peter F. Drucker, *The Executive in Action*, HarperBusiness, 1996

Philip B. Crosby, *The Eternally Successful Organization*, McGraw Hill Book Company, New York, 1988

R. D. Buzzel and B. T. Gale *The PIMS Principles: Linking Strategy to Performance,* The Free Press, New York, 1987

Robert Spector and Patrick D. McCarthy, *The Nordstrom Way: The Inside Story of America's #1 Customer Service Company*, Second Edition, John Wiley & Sons, Inc., 2000

Stephen S. Covey, *The 7 Habits of Highly Effective People*, Simon & Schuster, New York, 1989

Stephen S. Covey, *Living the 7 Habits: Stories of Courage and Inspiration*, Simon & Schuster, New York, 1999

Thisday, Tuesday, December 12, 2006

Thomas J. Peters and Robert H. Waterman Jr., *In Search of Excellence, Lessons From America's Best-Run Companies*, Harper & Row, New York, 1982

Thomas J. Peters and Nancy K. Austin, *A Passion For Excellence: The Leadership Difference*, Warner Books, New York, 1986.

Tom Peters, *Thriving on Chaos: Handbook for A Management Revolution,* Harper & Row Publishers, New York, 1988

Tom Peters, *Liberation Management: Necessary Disorganization for the Nanosecond Nineties* Alfred A. Knopf, 1992

Tom Peters, *The Circle of Innovation: You Can't Shrink Your Way to Greatness*, Vintage Book, 1999

Tom Peters, *The Pursuit of WOW! Crazy Times Call for Crazy Organizations* and *Tom Peters Seminar, BCA, London, 2000*

Tony Ansell *Approaches to Quality Management: Putting it Into Practice at the Local Level*: In the book *Financial Services*: *The Search for Quality*, Seminar Proceedings, The Chartered Institute of Bankers, London, 1993

Wayne Barrett, *Trump: The Deals and the Downfall*, Harper Collins, 1992

William H. Davidow and Bro Uttal, *Total Customer Service: The Ultimate Weapon*, Harper Perennial, New York, 1989